TEACHING READING IN
MULTILINGUAL CLASSROOMS

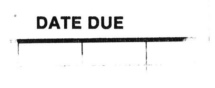

DATE DUE

David E. Freeman

Yvonne S. Freeman

HEINEM.
PORTSMOUT. .н

Heinemann

A division of Reed Elsevier, Inc.
361 Hanover Street
Portsmouth, NH 03801-3912
www.heinemann.com

Offices and agents throughout the world

Library of Congress Cataloging-in-Publication Data
CIP data is on file with the Library of Congress.
ISBN: 0-325-00248-7

Editor: Lois Bridges
Production: Michael Cirone
Cover and text design: Jeff Wincapaw
Manufacturing: Louise Richardson

Printed in the United States of America on acid-free paper

04   03   02   01   DA   2   3   4   5

We dedicate this book to all teachers commited to using the best approaches for teaching multilingual, multicultural students, including three dedicated teachers in our immediate family: our daughters, Mary and Ann, and our son-in-law, Francisco.

Contents

Acknowledgments

During our thirteen years as teacher educators in the Central Valley of California, we have had the privilege of observing and working with many outstanding teachers. We wish to acknowledge the contributions of these talented educators, who draw on the rich diversity in their classrooms to create exemplary learning communities. In this book we share their stories.

We would especially like to acknowledge Debbie Manning, whose teaching has provided demonstrations for teachers from not only Fresno but from all over the country. Debbie and our university colleague, Jean Fennacy, work together doing collaborative classroom research that informs them about how Debbie's students learn and informs future teachers about how they should respond to students as they teach.

Mike Lebsock draws on his special talents with art and computers encouraging his multilingual students to become proficient readers and writers through various ways of knowing, including drama, music, video, and crafts.

Sandra Mecuri, herself a recent immigrant from Argentina, has taught us how important it is to value students and have a positive impact on their futures, especially for those newcomers with no previous schooling. She gives of her talents, despite her own difficulty living in a country that is not her native land, because she knows she has been given much.

Cheri Hudson-Freeman has taught special needs students in Maine for many years with the patience and understanding of a true professional. She is constantly searching for the best way to meet her students' needs, and her creative units encourage her students to push themselves to reach their full potential.

Mary Soto, a high school ESL and drama teacher, and Francisco Soto, a third grade bilingual teacher, are fairly new teachers who have combined their passion for justice with their own personalities in developing their teaching philosophy and style. Ann Freeman has been both a bilingual elementary teacher and resource teacher. Like the Sotos, Ann has tried to meet the needs of Latino students with curriculum that draws on student strengths, empowering them through the reading of culturally-relevant literature and interesting content books.

Other teachers have provided additional valuable examples for this book. Erin English and Janet Calandra, both new teachers learning about second-language acquisition and methodology, applied what they were learning and showed how much children can and do learn when support-ed. Tom Thomas, an experienced and talented teacher from Michigan, shared with us his commitment to second-language teaching through the creative work of his students, Maya, Ronak, and Renee. Grace Klassen, another experienced and talented teacher, has taught and inspired Central Valley junior high students for some time.

Finally, we wish to thank our editor, Lois Bridges. We appreciate her experience and knowledge of both reading and teaching. We know that our writing always receives her careful consideration. The manuscript we first presented to her some months ago has evolved into this book because of her thoughtful suggestions and comments.

Introduction

Reading has become a hot topic. Newspapers trumpet reading test score results. Politicians campaign on reading reform. And educators scramble to keep pace with the latest plans to reform the teaching of reading. A great effort has been made to retrain teachers and enforce new policies for reading instruction, but little attention has been given to clarifying the goals of reading instruction or to giving teachers principles they can use to work effectively with an increasingly diverse student population.

Janet, a new fourth grade teacher working with a class of twenty-seven students, including twelve English-language learners, describes how she feels about teaching literacy in the present climate:

> Before I had my own class, I had this abstract idea that all children will learn because I know how to teach. What I didn't know was that not only is each child different, but each child's social and learning situation is different. It is impossible for anyone who has never been in a teaching position to know how difficult, demanding, and rewarding teaching can be. As so many people sit back and judge teachers and teaching methods and programs, they don't have any idea of what it's like to look in children's eyes and see the confusion and dismay they face when learning English and trying to make sense of what they are reading.

When asked, many teachers like Janet admit they are confused about the different strategies and approaches they are being asked to use with every child. Inservices about how reading must be taught include information on phonemic awareness and the development of fluency in reading. Materials provided often emphasize the importance of decodable texts. But seldom do trainers or publishers explain what instruction and materials are appropriate, when, and for whom. Are mandated programs right for all beginning readers? Struggling readers? Older readers? English language learners? These questions are especially perplexing for teachers, like Janet, who are working in multilingual classrooms.

Teaching in Multilingual Classrooms

Teachers face a variety of challenges as they plan reading instruction. Below, we briefly sketch the class settings of eight other teachers working in multilingual classrooms, and whose effective reading practices we describe in the subsequent chapters of this book.

Veronica

Veronica is a first grade teacher in a large, independent school district on the outskirts of a city in Texas. Although Veronica was trained as a Spanish/English bilingual teacher and her first years of teaching were with all native Spanish speakers, her classroom population has now changed. Growth in industry in the area, which was once more agricultural, has brought increased diversity to her school. Her students now include children whose parents are from Vietnam, Cambodia, and India.

Because of the multiple first languages in her classroom, Veronica provides most of her instruction in English, working hard to make the class comprehensible for all. Each school district determines exactly how bilingual students are served, but state regulations require that standardized tests be given to all students. Therefore, Veronica knows that her students will be tested in English. Pressures from the school district and state agencies push her towards an emphasis on teaching for the test, but Veronica is not convinced that that will give her students long-term academic success. She doesn't just want her multilingual students to pass reading tests. She wants them to become independent readers.

Debbie

Debbie teaches a multiage first-through-third-grade class in a school that once educated middle class children, but now serves an inner city population of primarily low-income families. Debbie began this year with twenty children from extremely diverse cultural, social, and economic backgrounds. Two of the children in the class are siblings of Chinese descent, three are African Americans, and six are of Mexican descent. One of the Hispanic children is still struggling with English. Several of the children have had a history of creating discipline problems for other teachers, and two take Ritalin during the day. Several children are from single-parent homes or are living with grandparents. Others have been traumatized by various experiences: two children saw their mother murdered, and one child was homeless for some time.

Debbie's classroom is print-rich, full of children's literature and her students' work. Her goal is to create a community of learners who take charge of their own learning. Debbie draws upon what she knows about literacy and her own students' needs and works to help them become independent readers, writers, speakers, and thinkers, against odds that seem to constantly challenge them outside her classroom.

Mary

Mary is presently a high school ESL and drama teacher. For her first two years, she taught in a high school in a rural farming community with Latino and Punjabi students. She is now teaching in a larger coastal community, where the high school population of 3,000 is 90 percent Hispanic.

Mary is a credentialed Spanish/English bilingual secondary teacher. Because she understands second-language acquisition and has training in bilingual and ESL methodology, she organizes her classroom and activities in ways that help students build on their strengths, including their first language and culture, in order to succeed. This year, Mary is teaching one drama course in Spanish, and students in her class are reading and writing plays in Spanish. The major drama production she is directing this year is a play that celebrates the accomplishments of Latina women. In her classes Mary puts special emphasis on the importance of reading, as well as providing access to reading materials that are engaging and relevant.

Francisco

Francisco is a third grade teacher in a California coastal town. His first two years of teaching were spent in a rural farming community in central California, where his bilingual classroom was filled mainly with migrant children. This year, Francisco's students include migrant children and children of parents settled in the community and working in agriculture or other industries. In his first school, he was teaching in a bilingual setting. Now he is teaching in a district where the administration encourages English-only instruction, so his classroom also includes some native English speakers.

Francisco is aware of the importance of primary-language literacy for long-term academic success, but he must also find ways to help his students feel confident as readers and writers in English. He must, therefore, organize his curriculum in a meaningful way that is comprehensible to his students and that will help them compete academically in English in the future.

Ann

Ann is a Title I reading resource specialist in a charter school in an Arizona border town. This K–12 school, located in converted homes and clinics in a barrio, has around 150 students. Almost all the students come from high-poverty-level homes and are on free lunch. The school has received funding to provide a two-way bilingual program for all grades. The students include both native Spanish speakers and native English speakers.

Teachers in the school are all fluent in Spanish, and some received their teacher training in Mexico. The entire school has adopted the theme "Who Am I?" in order to encourage students to develop a strong sense of self and belief in their potential as learners. Because the school is new and teachers come from varied backgrounds, Ann has had several daunting tasks. She has had to organize bilingual reading resources, including a library. Because teachers in a two-way program have some students learning in a language that is not their native language at all times, she has worked with teachers on second-language teaching strategies and techniques. In addition, few of the teachers have had training in how to teach reading, so Ann has begun inservice training on teaching reading in both Spanish and English.

Cheri

Cheri is a sixth, seventh, and eighth grade Resource teacher in a middle school in the largest metropolitan area in Maine. Her students are assigned to her classroom for a variety of reasons: Some have been identified as having mild retardation; some have health impairments; some have been identified as being learning disabled; some are mildly depressed; some have emotional or behavioral problems and receive prescription drugs such as Ritalin during the day; and some have been diagnosed with speech and language disorders. While all of Cheri's students are mainstreamed for part of the day, they do about half of their core course work in her classroom. A few stay with her for all their core classes. Her class size is fifteen students, but there are usually eleven or fewer in the classroom at any time. This constant movement of students during the day challenges Cheri to organize her curriculum so that students coming in and out will be able use their time with her constructively and be ready to join her learning community without too much interruption.

In the past few years, Cheri and other teachers in her community have seen more English-language learners appear in their classrooms. For example, in the last two years, there have been students whose native languages were Farsi (Iran), Khmer (Cambodia), Somali, Vietnamese, Acholi (Sudan), Russian, Serbo-Croatian, French, and Spanish. Cheri knows that the presence of second-language learners brings further complexity to her already-complex classroom. She and other teachers in the district have begun to attend workshops on how to work effectively with bilingual students. This year, as in recent years, Cheri has an English learner in class, a Cambodian student whose first language is Khmer.

Cheri's goal for her students is to prepare them to function successfully in the mainstream. In order to do that, she must help them learn how to learn. She knows that as her students begin to experience some success, they will be greater risk-takers and will be more likely to improve academically.

Sandra

Sandra, a bilingual Spanish/English teacher, works with fourth, fifth, and sixth graders in a rural farming community in California. Her students, who are almost all newcomers to this country, speak Spanish or Mixteco, a native dialect of southern Mexico. They arrive here with little to no previous schooling. Few are literate in their first language. Her students have little confidence in themselves as learners.

Since many of the children are from migrant families, their schooling, once they start studying in the United States, is often interrupted. Work takes families to states to the north from May to early October, and family obligations take them back to Mexico in November and December. Sandra's challenge, then, is to provide these students with the literacy skills and concept development they have missed and give them enough academic English to survive in junior high and high school.

Mike

Mike teaches fifth grade in a school that, even though it is located on the edge of the city, still has an inner-city population of students, many of whom are living at the poverty level. Students at the school are from multiple cultural backgrounds. Mike has students from Mexico, from the Middle East, including Iraq and Iran, from India and Pakistan, and from the Balkans, Ukraine, Russia, and Yugoslavia. Most of the students speak and understand English fairly well, but not all do.

At Mike's school site, upper grade teachers rotate their classes. Last year,

Mike taught nearly one hundred different students in his three science classes. This year, Mike is working with three classes teaching writing using a writers workshop format. He also has his homeroom group of around thirty students long enough to work with them on literature studies. Mike sees that one of his biggest challenges is to help all of his students become competent readers and writers. He believes this is best done in community, but the constant rotation of students makes it more difficult for Mike to build the kind of community needed to meet the needs of his diverse students.

All eight of these teachers have been impacted by recent changes in student population. In Chapter One, we examine the demographic shifts that have so dramatically influenced all aspects of teaching, including the teaching of reading. We then introduce a Checklist for Effective Reading Instruction that teachers can use to help all students develop literacy. We conclude with an extended example from Veronica's class to show how she plans and evaluates her reading curriculum by using the Checklist.

In the following chapters, we outline the theory of reading that underlies the Checklist and discuss each item on the Checklist, giving examples of how the principles for effective reading instruction work in multilingual contexts—that is, in classrooms like those described above, with a few or many English-language learners. In the final chapter, "Answering the Hard Questions About Reading," we address the questions about phonemic awareness, phonics, decodable texts, teaching vocabulary, and other difficult issues that teachers face.

Checklist for Effective Reading Instruction

Changing Demographics

One factor that has strongly impacted all teaching, and especially the teaching of reading, is the rapid shift in student population that has occurred across the United States and Canada in recent years. Our schools reflect an increasingly rich linguistic diversity, and this brings with it a challenge for teachers because many more students at all grade levels have limited English proficiency.

Data from the National Clearinghouse on Bilingual Education (NCBE) reflect a tremendous growth in the number of Limited English Proficent (LEP) students in the United States. Between 1989 and 2000, for example, the general school population, K–12, grew by about 5.5 million students. This represents a 13.6 percent increase. During the same period, the number of students classified as LEP rose from about two million to over four million, an increase of over 100 percent. In 1989, LEP students represented about 5 percent of the total school population, and by 2000 they account for nearly 9 percent of all students.

English learners are not concentrated in one area of the country. The five states with the greatest number of LEP students are California, Florida, Illinois, New York, and Texas. All five of these states have identified more than 100,000 students as limited English proficient. Teachers everywhere face the challenge of teaching reading to students whose English proficiency is limited. English learners make up more than 10 percent of the school population in Alaska, Arizona, California, Florida, New Mexico, and Texas. Even in states like Montana, North Dakota, and Rhode Island, the number of students who are classified as LEP is between 5 and 10 percent (NCBE).

California has the highest number of LEP students. The statistics for 1998 show the following:

♦ 1,442,692 LEP students out of a K–12 population of 5.7 million.

♦ 25 percent of the total K-12 school population are English learners.

♦ 2.6 percent increase from the previous year.

♦ 254 percent increase from 1986.

Several of the teachers whose classes we describe in this book work in the Central Valley of California, where student demographics have shifted rapidly as in many other areas across the country.

♦ Between 1988 and 1996 the LEP population of Fresno County schools increased 109 percent.

♦ English learners now represent 57.4 percent of the total school enrollment.

The California numbers are especially high, and that, in part, is because the total state population is high. However, the growth of LEP students as a percentage of the school population is lower in California than in many other states. Between 1990 and 1997, for example, twelve states had a greater than 200 percent increase in LEP students. These states include Alabama, Alaska, Arkansas, Florida, Idaho, Kansas, Kentucky, Nebraska, Nevada, North Carolina, Oklahoma, and Oregon. Another nine states experienced between 100 and 200 percent growth of English learners. During that same period, California was only one of fourteen states whose LEP population increased between 50 and 100 percent (NCBE).

Teachers like those described in the Introduction, who work in multilingual classrooms, are faced with the challenge of implementing new ways to teach reading with some or many students whose English proficiency is limited, and whose background knowledge and experiences are very different from the characters in the stories they are asked to read. To ensure that their students develop the literacy they need, teachers need guidelines for effective practices they can use to promote literacy development for all their students.

In the following section, we offer a set of guidelines in the form of a Checklist for Effective Reading Instruction (Freeman and Freeman, 1997). We do not pretend to have the magic pill, the solution to all the reading woes we read about in academic journals, papers, and magazines. In fact, we question the bleak picture of reading that the newspapers often paint (see McQuillan's *The Literacy Crisis*, 1998). But we have confidence in the

Checklist for Effective Reading Instruction

1. Do students value themselves as readers, and do they value reading?

2. Do students read from a wide variety of genres?

3. Do students see teachers engaged in reading for pleasure as well as for information?

4. Do students have a wide variety of reading materials to choose from and time to read?

5. Do students make good choices in their reading?

6. Do students regard reading as meaning making at all times? That is, do they construct meaning as they read?

7. Are students effective readers? That is, do they make a balanced use of all three cueing systems?

8. Are students efficient readers? That is, do they make minimal use of cues to construct meaning?

9. Are students provided with appropriate strategy lessons if they experience difficulties in their reading?

10. Do students have opportunities to talk about what they have read, making connections between the reading and their own experiences?

11. Do students revise their individual understandings of texts in response to the comments of classmates?

12. Is there evidence that students' writing is influenced by what they read?

Figure 1–1 Checklist for Effective Reading Instruction

professionalism of teachers, and we believe that if they follow certain basic principles, they can help all of their students become proficient readers.

Checklist for Effective Reading Instruction

We have developed a Checklist for Effective Reading Instruction (see Fig. 1–1) that we invite teachers, reading specialists, curriculum developers, and administrators to use as they plan and evaluate reading lessons and programs for all their students.

In the chapters that follow, we will discuss each of the questions on the Checklist in detail. We hope that readers will use the practical suggestions we offer and learn from the classroom scenarios we present to illustrate points from the Checklist. Our goal will be accomplished if readers of this book are able to use the Checklist to evaluate and refine the way they teach reading.

In the next section, we provide an example of one teacher who teaches reading effectively. This teacher has developed a reading curriculum that follows the Checklist.

Literacy Through a Content Theme: "What About Bugs?"

In the introduction, we described Veronica as a first grade teacher working in a multilingual classroom. To help her students become competent readers and writers, Veronica organizes her curriculum around themes (Freeman and Freeman, 1998). Figure 1–2 lists some of the reasons why this is beneficial for English language learners.

Because her students speak several different languages, Veronica teaches mainly in English. She is able to preview lessons in Spanish when working in small groups with her Spanish-speaking students, and she has gathered some resources in Spanish. But she has few resources in Vietnamese, Khmer, or the several Indian dialects of her other bilingual students. Her unit on bugs is an example of how she carefully chooses activities and materials that help her students develop academic concepts and linguistic proficiency by using a theme as a central focus.

Veronica knew that she wanted to use a theme that would interest all her students, and in which all students would have some background. She also knew she needed to work on developing her students' reading profi-

▲ Students see the big picture so they can make sense of English language instruction
▲ Content areas (math, science, social studies, literature) are interrelated
▲ Vocabulary is repeated naturally as it appears in different content area studies
▲ Through themes based on big questions, teachers can connect curriculum to students' lives, making curriculum more interesting
▲ Because the curriculum makes sense, English-language learners are more fully-engaged and experience more success
▲ Since themes deal with universal human topics, all students can be involved, and lessons and activities can be adjusted to different levels of English language proficiency

Figure 1–2 Reasons to Organize Curriculum Around Themes

ciency, especially in reading content-area books. In the following section, we describe the initial activities in a unit Veronica developed around "bugs." Then, we evaluate the unit with the Checklist for Effective Reading Instruction.

Launching the "What About Bugs?" Unit

Veronica began by singing with the children two favorite songs many of them remembered from kindergarten: "The Itsy Bitsy Spider" (Trapani, 1996) and the counting song, "One Elephant, Two Elephants" (Wainman, 1982), a fanciful song about elephants on a spider web. She wrote the words on large song sheets and clipped the songs to her standing song chart. The children sang the songs together as a student volunteer tracked the words on the song sheet. Veronica also asked the Spanish speakers if they knew the song in Spanish, "Los elefantes," which is similar to the elephant song in English, but has a different tune. Since some students were familiar with the song in Spanish, Veronica put the words up on the song sheet, too, and the whole class sang it in Spanish, led by the Spanish speakers and accompanied by a tape (Ada, 1991).

Veronica then asked the students what the songs had in common. The children immediately called out, "spiders." Next, Veronica asked the students what they knew about spiders and wrote down student responses as they called out their answers. "They are bugs." "They can bite you." "I don't like spiders." "They eat flies." "They make webs." "Baby spiders come from eggs." After the students talked about spiders for a while, Veronica read them *The Very Busy Spider* (Carle, 1984). All the students wanted to feel the raised spider web on each page, so Veronica allowed one student to come up each time the page was turned. The children talked about the spider web catching the fly at the end of the story. When they talked about spiders and flies, Veronica asked them what the two had in common. "They are bugs!" several children replied. For the next day, Veronica asked the students to try to find a bug and bring it to school in a jar with twigs and leaves. She suggested that the students ask for help from their parents to be sure none would get stung or bitten.

The next day, several students brought in bugs to show. Some had beetles; some had ants; others had caterpillars or crickets. One student brought in a moth; one had a butterfly; two had ladybugs; and one had a bee. Veronica then read to them *Have You Seen Bugs?* (Oppenheim, 1996), a delightful book in rhyme about bugs. The book explains where bugs are found, what they eat, and how they reproduce. She asked the students to think about where they found their bugs and if their bugs were like the ones discussed in the book. After the reading, the children brought up their bugs during share time and told how and where they caught them. Many of the children connected their experience to the book Veronica had just read. Veronica wrote the kind of bug each child had found on a large strip of paper. She and the students talked about the first letter of the words and different sounds they heard when saying them. For example, Veronica explained, "'Bee' has the same first sound as 'beetle.' Do you notice any other letters that are the same in 'bee' and 'beetle'?" If students had bugs that were in *The Icky Bug Alphabet Book* (Palotta, 1986), another resource book, Veronica read that page to the students. For example, ant, bumblebee, cricket, grasshopper, and moth were bugs featured on the pages for the letters *A*, *B*, *C*, *G*, and *M*.

Next, all the jars of bugs were placed on a table in front of the classroom, and the strips of paper with the bug names were laid out on a table. Veronica read the children three limited-text books in the Science for Emergent Readers series: *Bugs, Bugs, Bugs* (Reid and Chessen, 1998), *Where*

Do Insects Live? (Canizares and Reid, 1998), and *What Do Insects Do?* (Canizares and Chanko, 1998). These books are illustrated with large photographs of insects. The children were fascinated by the pictures and commented on the bugs they recognized. Since the text is limited and predictable, Veronica encouraged students to read the text along with her. Then she invited the students to read the books with her a second time, so everyone could think about the pictures, the words, and the information in the books.

Next, each child was asked to choose a bug to draw and write about. Veronica told the children they could look at the bugs in the jars or use the books she had read or other books about insects that she had in the room, to get ideas for their drawing and writing. She pointed out that she had several books in Spanish about insects, including one about ladybugs, *La mariquita* (Cappellini, 1993), one about flies, *La mosca* (Almada, 1993), and another about mosquitoes, *El mosquito* (Almada, 1993). Veronica showed the children the pictures in the books and told them they could all look at those pictures, and that maybe some Spanish speaker could help them if they wanted to read the books. She also announced that she was going to read a book in Spanish about amazing insects as they got started on their drawings, and anyone who was interested could come and listen.

As the students began their work, Veronica encouraged her three Spanish speakers to listen to *Insectos asombrosos* (*Amazing Insects*) (Kite, 1997) and was pleased when four other students in the class, including two Southeast-Asian children, also came to listen. For the Spanish speakers, this short book reinforced concepts already discussed, such as where insects live and how they eat. The non-Spanish speakers contributed to the reading by asking questions about the pictures.

As the children drew their bugs and labeled their pictures or wrote short sentences about their insects, they made important observations. Some students noticed that spiders have eight legs, but beetles, ants, bees, and butterflies have only six. Veronica put up large posters of an insect and a spider and discussed the difference in number of legs with all the children.

The next day Veronica began the day by inviting children to share their picture and what they wrote. Students hung their pictures around the room under letters of the alphabet; so ants were under *A*, and caterpillars and crickets were hung under *C*. Then Veronica took out the word strips she had made the day before and asked students to pin the large, printed words up under the letter of the alphabet the word started with. When they were finished, the student pictures and the large, printed insect words covered the wall under the alphabet.

At recess that day, several children had trouble finding their insects in the jars among the twigs and leaves. This brought up the concept of camouflage, so after lunch Veronica read *How to Hide a Butterfly* (Heller, 1985), *The Mixed-Up Chameleon* (Carle, 1989), *The Icky Bug Counting Book* (Pallota, 1992), and *The Big Bug Search* (Jackson, 1998)—books that show how insects are camouflaged in nature. The children loved finding the insects in the illustrations of leaves and branches. Next, Veronica brought out an old favorite, *The Very Hungry Caterpillar* (Carle, 1969). First, she did a "picture walk" through the book. She turned the pages and had students tell her what they saw and what they thought was happening. Picture walks help English-language learners build up vocabulary and help all students focus on the overall meaning of a story before they begin to read. Then, the whole class read the book together.

After reading the book, the children talked about how a caterpillar changes into a butterfly. Veronica took out a new story, *La mariposa* (*The Butterfly*) (Jiménez, 1998). She read the English version of the book (which retains the Spanish title). It tells the story of a first grade Hispanic boy who does not speak English. He is lonely at school. His only joy comes from watching a caterpillar in the classroom spin a cocoon and eventually emerge as a beautiful butterfly. The book had been read in Spanish to her Spanish speakers by a parent volunteer the afternoon before. In discussion, many of the children in the class related to the loneliness of the non-English speaker. Veronica then showed the class a caterpillar that she had brought in a jar and explained that over the next few weeks, they would watch the caterpillar change into a butterfly, just as Francisco in the story did.

Another butterfly book that Veronica showed the students was *The Butterfly Alphabet* (Sandved, 1996). The author has taken photographs of butterflies all over the world. By taking closeups of butterfly wings, he has been able to include patterns that represent each of the letters in the alphabet. As Veronica read the poetry on each page, she showed the class the page, and they identified the alphabet letter on the wing. During shared reading time that day, Veronica put out a variety of books for students to read, including the camouflage books and *The Butterfly Alphabet*. She also displayed *The Butterfly Counting Book* (Pallotta, 1998) and some more-limited-text books, like *Butterfly* (Canizares, 1998) and *The Tiny Dot* (Whitney, 1996), for students to read together and discuss. As she moved about the room, she was excited to see how involved all her students were in reading and discussing the books.

Figure 1–3 lists the books Veronica used in this unit.

Ada, Alma Flor. 1991. *Días y días de poesía*. Carmel, Calif.: Hampton Brown.

Almada, Pat. 1993. *El mosquito*. Crystal Lake, Ill.: Rigby.

———. 1993. *La mosca*. Crystal Lake, Ill.: Rigby.

Canizares, Susan. 1998. *Butterfly*. New York: Scholastic.

Canizares, Susan, and Pamela Chanko. 1998. *What Do Insects Do?* New York: Scholastic.

Canizares, Susan, and Mary Reid. 1998. *Where Do Insects Live?* New York: Scholastic.

Cappellini, Mary. 1993. *La mariquita*. Crystal Lake, Ill.: Rigby.

Carle, Eric. 1989. *The Mixed-Up Chameleon*. New York: Scholastic.

———. 1984. *The Very Busy Spider*. New York: Scholastic.

———. 1969. *The Very Hungry Caterpillar*. Cleveland: The World Publishing Company.

Dussling, Jennifer. 1998. *Bugs! Bugs! Bugs!* New York: DK Publishing.

Facklam, Margery. 1999. *Bugs for Lunch*. New York: Scholastic.

Florian, Douglas. 1998. *Insectlopedia*. New York: Scholastic.

Heller, Ruth. 1985. *How To Hide A Butterfly And Other Insects*. New York: Grosset and Dunlap.

Jackson, Ian. 1998. *The Big Bug Search*. New York: Scholastic.

Jiménez, Francisco. 1998. *La mariposa*. Boston: Houghton Mifflin.

Kite, Patricia. 1997. *Insectos asombrosos*. Boston: Houghton Mifflin.

Oppenheim, Joanne. 1996. *Have You Seen Bugs?* New York: Scholastic.

Pallotta, Jerry. 1998. *The Butterfly Counting Book*. New York: Scholastic.

———. 1986. *The Icky Bug Alphabet Book*. New York: Scholastic.

———. 1992. *The Icky Bug Counting Book*. New York: Scholastic.

Reid, Mary, and Betsey Chessen. 1998. *Bugs, Bugs, Bugs* (Science Emergent Readers). New York: Scholastic.

Sandved, Kjell B. 1996. *The Butterfly Alphabet*. New York: Scholastic.

Trapani, Iza. 1996. *The Itsy Bitsy Spider*. Boston: Houghton Mifflin.

Wainman, Margaret. 1982. *One Elephant, Two Elephants*. Port Coquitlam, Canada: Class Size Books.

Whitney, Natalie. 1996. *The Tiny Dot*. Boston: Houghton Mifflin.

Figure 1–3 "What About Bugs?" Unit Bibliography

Evaluating the Unit with the Checklist for Effective Reading Instruction

Using the Checklist to review the activities Veronica used to launch her theme shows that she has developed an effective reading program.

♦ She included a large variety of activities so that all her students could come to value reading and value themselves as readers.

♦ Veronica's students read both content area texts and literature, including songs, poems, and stories, several times each day.

♦ Veronica also read to her students every day so they could see how she enjoyed reading.

♦ The students had constant access to a wide variety of books to satisfy the curiosity that was stimulated by each day's activities.

♦ Veronica helped students at different proficiency levels choose books they could read and enjoy.

♦ By organizing around a theme, Veronica kept the focus of reading on constructing meaning.

♦ Veronica's students are on their way to becoming efficient and effective readers. Even when Veronica was helping them focus on beginning sounds and letters, she connected this to the content they were learning. Bringing in *The Butterfly Alphabet* made that connection even stronger. Veronica also planned strategy lessons, including reading to students with limited English in their native language, helping students predict words, and doing a picture walk.

♦ Even at this beginning level, students were encouraged to read, write, and share their ideas relating what was being read to what they were learning about bugs.

Through careful selection of materials, close observation of her students, and an understanding of how literacy develops, Veronica supported the first graders with her effective reading program. In the next chapter, we examine in more detail the theory of reading that supports the practices that Veronica and other effective teachers follow.

Understanding Reading 2

Introduction

The Checklist for Effective Reading Instruction is based on a specific theory of reading. Teachers who implement the Checklist understand reading so they can explain why they teach the way they do. Their classrooms and their daily schedules are organized to provide the experiences all students need to become proficient readers. In this chapter, we look at one teacher whose reading curriculum is consistent with the Checklist. We begin by describing her classroom and her daily schedule and go on to explain the view of reading that forms the basis for her teaching practices.

Debbie's Class

Debbie was introduced in the Introduction as a teacher who works with a very diverse group of students, many of whom have not had positive experiences with reading and writing in the past. Debbie has a master's degree in reading and many years of classroom experience. In addition, she has a passion for and a knowledge of children's literature. In fact, she is part owner of a children's bookstore and teaches a university course about children's literature. All of these factors have influenced how Debbie sets up the daily routine for her students.

The room in which Debbie teaches has tables (rather than desks), a rug section, a reading loft, shelves, cupboards, counters under the windows and along some of the walls, and lots of books. Around the room, there are animals to be cared for, science projects in various stages, charts, graphs, a working radio station, a typewriter, several computers, resource materials such as telephone books and maps, and lots of the children's work. There are almost always several adults in the room. There is often an aide, but there is also usually a student teacher, a parent or two, a university researcher, and/or students from other classrooms who serve as tutors.

Since Debbie's is a multiage classroom, she often organizes responsibilities around age and experience. The "olders" are the third graders, who have been with her the longest. The "middlers" are the second graders, and the "youngers" are the first graders, who are spending their first year in her room. Debbie's assignments fit the needs of her students. Shy students might be asked to work with a more confident partner, or an aggressive child might be asked to collect information in a quiet, nonviolent way. A look at Debbie's schedule shows that she provides many opportunities for all her students to develop as proficient readers. This schedule promotes all the practices consistent with the Checklist for Effective Reading Instruction.

Debbie's Daily Schedule

8:00–8:20—Socialization Time—Olders help youngers sign in and find their name tags. They find out who has hot or cold lunch and help youngers read the list of what they will need to prepare for that day, which usually includes picking books to read during Readers Workshop. These olders are responsible for reporting the absences and the lunch count—a challenging addition-and-subtraction math activity, as the sum must equal the number of children in the class. During this time, students help each other and talk about what happened at home or in school the previous day and what's coming up. Often, comments such as, "I'm going to start a new story today" or "Oh, that's a good book. You'll like it!" are heard.

8:20–8:30—Two olders call the other children to the rug. They ask the children if they have anything they want to share. Volunteers share briefly. Two olders read the weather report, which they have written by looking at the newspaper in the room as well as actually looking outside. One older reads a story math problem he has chosen, then leads the others in the solution, using a white board if necessary. A middler assigns who will be in the special positions, including the reading loft, big book section, and listening center, during reading time.

8:30–9:00—Debbie reads one to three books for discussion. She chooses books that fit different grade levels and personalities. Often, the books are on a theme that the class has been discussing. At times, she also focuses on words, letters, and sounds and does linguistic studies with the children.

9:00–10:00—Readers Workshop—Debbie's goal is to get all the children to read independently. In this segment, she goes around and listens to them read, noticing who is struggling with what. At the beginning of the year, Debbie and other adults in the room note things such as which children are only reading pictures; which children are reading out loud correctly but not getting any meaning; or which children are choosing books that are too hard or too easy. This information helps Debbie form groups for mini-lessons that fit their needs. Eventually, she organizes literature study groups. Initially, these begin with a group of 6–8 proficient readers. Later, she expands the groups to include more children, as they become ready to engage in conversations about books that they read themselves or that their parents or a teacher read to them.

10:00–10:15—All the children record in their reading journals three books they read during Readers Workshop. They categorize the books as easy, just right, or challenging. They also write a specific response to one of the books, going back to reread one or more pages to tell why they are writing about that part. Beginning readers are encouraged to find a page, describe what happened on that page, hold that sentence description in their head, and write what they are thinking the best they can.

10:15–10:30—Recess

10:30–11:00—Debbie reads again to the class, and they discuss the reading. She chooses a different genre from the earlier reading, and often chooses a chapter book.

11:00–12:00—Writers Workshop—During this time, Debbie's goal is to help all her students become independent writers. They choose their own topics, and Debbie encourages them to try different kinds of writing. They write stories or ads, math problems or science information pieces. She and other adults give the students strategies for spelling and other mini-lessons, as needed. Once Debbie knows the children, she pulls aside small groups and works with them on areas they struggle with. She often uses the overhead or a white board to show the students all kinds of writing, from newspaper articles to magazine articles to ads, and they discuss how to read and write those kinds of pieces. Sometimes, she gives them photocopies to read as a class or take home. Students can use the computer for word processing. Debbie calls beginning writers aside and does Language Experience, in which they dictate a story to her, she writes or types it on the computer, and then makes copies for the group to read in unison. Later, the students as a group read the story to the whole class.

12:00–12:35—Lunch

12:35–1:00—Reading and mini-lessons. During this time, Debbie focuses on nonfiction reading in the areas of math, science, and history and does writing mini-lessons.

1:00–2:30—Inquiry. During this time, students and teacher together carry out inquiry projects of mutual interest. Working in small groups, they explore math, science, and social studies concepts. They read and interpret data, representing their findings on charts and graphs, and report their findings to their classmates. They continually read, discuss, interpret, and share information.

Debbie's curriculum is built on a strong knowledge base. She has a clear understanding of how her students learn, particularly of how they learn to read. As a result, she can explain to parents and administrators why she teaches the way she does. Her experiences, coupled with her studies, have convinced her that her students acquire literacy as she reads to and with them, and then as they read independently. In the rest of this chapter, we explain the theories of language acquisition and reading that provide the basis for Debbie's teaching.

Learning and Acquisition

Teachers in multilingual classrooms know that many of their students need to develop both English proficiency and reading proficiency. For that reason, they base their teaching on current language acquisition theory. Krashen (1982) has developed a theory of second-language acquisition that holds that developing a second language is much like developing a first language. An important distinction that Krashen makes is between *acquiring* a language and *learning* one. Figure 2–1 highlights some of the differences between learning and acquisition.

Learning	Aquisition
▲ Conscious	▲ Subconscious
▲ Occurs in formal contexts	▲ Occurs in formal or informal contexts
▲ Results from direct teaching	▲ Results from trying to communicate
▲ Involves learning rules	▲ Involves using language for real purposes
▲ Can be tested	▲ Can be used

Figure 2–1 Learning and Acquisition

If you studied a foreign language in high school or college, you probably experienced *learning*. We learn a language in formal contexts, like classrooms, as the result of direct teaching. We study the rules and memorize vocabulary. Learning is a conscious process that usually involves presentation of the parts of the language, practice using those parts, and testing to determine mastery.

On the other hand, if you picked up some Spanish when you went to Mexico on vacation, you *acquired* language. Acquisition is a subconscious process. We are not aware that we are acquiring vocabulary and grammar. Acquisition most often occurs in informal situations such as when we order a meal in a restaurant, shop for souvenirs, or ask directions. However, acquisition also occurs in classrooms in which teachers create interesting lessons that involve students in authentic language use. Acquisition happens when we are involved in real communication. We pick up language as we attempt to understand and produce meaningful messages—as we use language for real purposes.

Unfortunately, most of us who have studied a second language in high school or college are not very proficient. David's four years of learning French did not prepare him to travel to France and carry on daily activities. In contrast, David lived in Colombia, Mexico, and Venezuela at different times, and during those stays, he acquired enough Spanish to function reasonably well with that language.

Acquisition leads to proficiency in a language. Teachers can observe this with new immigrant students who come to school speaking little English. In a short time, these students pick up the language they need for basic communication. They can function in English, in and out of school, even though they may make grammatical errors and may speak with an accent. These students are acquiring conversational English. However, these same students may struggle in their academic classes. Extensive research (Collier 1992; Cummins 1996) has shown that it takes much longer to acquire the academic language of school than the language of everyday communication. This is because students are exposed to great amounts of conversational language in and out of school, but they receive much less exposure to the academic language of books, essays, and tests needed for school success. As a result, academic language proficiency is acquired more slowly than conversational proficiency.

Comprehensible Input

The key to acquisition is receiving messages we understand, what Krashen calls "comprehensible input." This is what happens when we understand directions in a foreign country and actually get where we hoped to go. Every time we understand a message, we acquire a bit more of the new language. Comprehensible input activates the parts of the brain that lead to language development.

Krashen (1993, 1996, 1999) has extended his theory of acquisition to include literacy. He argues that we acquire the ability to read and write in the same way we acquire a second language. In the case of reading, the input comes from written language. Teachers make the input comprehensible when they read to students from big books or song or poetry charts. As students follow along, they begin to make connections between the oral reading and the print. Eventually, they acquire enough knowledge of written language to read on their own. To understand how this process works, we need to look in more detail at a theory of reading that is consistent with Krashen's theory of language acquisition.

A Sociopsycholinguistic Theory of Reading

In the same way that people need to receive comprehensible input to acquire a new language, they need to make sense of texts to acquire reading proficiency. The process of developing reading proficiency is both social and psychological. Reading, like all language processes, is social because it involves communication with others. Children learn to read by interacting with other people. Reading is also social because, when readers construct meaning, they bring their background knowledge and experiences to the text. This background includes social factors, such as the reader's values and culture. These social factors may strongly influence the meaning a reader constructs from a text.

At the same time, reading is an individual, psychological process that involves language. A sociopsycholinguistic theory accounts for the social, psychological, and linguistic factors involved in reading. In the following sections, we outline a sociopsycholinguistic theory of reading. We begin by defining reading. Then we look at the kind of cues readers use to construct meaning. Finally, we consider the steps involved in reading. A considerable body of research supports this meaning-centered theory of reading. Figure 2–2 includes some of the key research.

Braunger, J. and J. Lewis. 1997. *Building a Knowledge Base in Reading.* Urbana, Ill.: NCTE.

Coles, G. 2000. *Misreading Reading: The Bad Science That Hurts Children.* Portsmouth, N.H.: Heinemann.

Dahl, K. 2000. *Teaching Phonics in Context.* Portsmouth, N.H.: Heinemann.

Elley, W. 1991. "Acquiring Literacy in a Second Language: The Effect of Book-Based Programs." *Language Learning* 41, (2): 403–439, 1991.

Ferreiro, E. and A. Teberosky. 1982. *Literacy Before Schooling.* Translated by Karen Goodman Castro. Portsmouth, N.H.: Heinemann.

Goodman, K. S. 1965. "Cues and Miscues in Reading: A Linguistic Study." *Elementary English* 42, (6): 635–642.

McQuillan, J. 1998. *The Literacy Crisis: False Claims, Real Solutions.* Portsmouth, N.H.: Heinemann.

Teale, W. and E. Sulzby, eds. 1986. *Emergent Literacy: Writing and Reading.* Norwood, N.J.: Ablex.

Figure 2–2 Research Supporting a Sociopsycholinguistic View of Reading

Constructing Meaning

We define reading as a process of constructing meaning from a text. Students who are learning to read need to understand that reading involves making sense of texts, rather than just pronouncing words. Constructing meaning involves using cues from the printed text and background knowledge, in a process that Rosenblatt (1978) calls a "transaction." According to Rosenblatt, the meaning is not in the words themselves, nor is it entirely in the reader's mind. Instead, meaning is constructed each time a reader and a text come together.

In any reading transaction, the text plays an important role. Texts have what Harste (1984) calls a "meaning potential." If I read "Little Red Riding Hood," for example, I can construct a variety of meanings, but some meanings are not possible. I probably wouldn't decide this was a story about a boy and his dog. In other words, what's in a text limits the possible meanings. At the same time, since a reader has certain background knowledge, there is a range of meanings that any individual can develop while reading a text. Second-language students may not have the same background experiences as mainstream students so it is not surprising that second-language students may develop different meanings from their classmates. However, the goal of reading instruction is to help all readers construct meaning by transacting with texts.

This idea of constructing meaning through transactions with text may seem pretty abstract, so let's take an example. Ads are texts. What meaning can you construct from "double coupons"? Is this a command to multiply the number of coupons by two? That's the meaning a second-language learner might construct. Menus are texts, too. What meaning do you construct from "an early bird special"? Can you imagine the confusion this can cause an English-language learner trying to read a menu? And are "early birds" the same as "snowbirds"? They might be, in Arizona. Readers with different backgrounds might construct quite different meanings from the same text. A young, Jewish reader who has lived all his life in New York City transacts differently with a Jan Karon novel about an aging Episcopal priest's adventures in the small southern town of Mitford (Karon, 1994) than a middle-aged, lifelong Episcopalian who was raised in a small rural community.

The Three Cue Systems

The reader's previous experiences, including experiences with texts, play an important role in meaning construction. The other source of meaning is the text. Readers use three kinds of text cues:

♦ Graphophonic cues

♦ Syntactic cues

♦ Semantic cues

Proficient readers make a balanced use of cues from all three cue systems to construct meaning. Readers use these text cues subconsciously, as they acquire reading proficiency in the process of reading. Teachers may present strategy lessons that highlight different cue systems, bringing aspects of the systems to conscious attention, but the underlying assumption is that readers will *acquire* control of the cue systems through reading, rather than *learning* them as the result of direct instruction. Below, we look at each of these three cue systems.

Graphophonic Cues

The term *graphophonics* comes from Goodman (1996) and refers to the combination of visual, sound, and phonic information readers use when they scan a text. Readers use visual information to identify letters and punctuation marks. This is their knowledge of orthography. They also use their understanding of the sounds of words. This is their knowledge of phonology. And they use their knowledge of phonics—the system that connects the patterns of letters with the patterns of sounds.

Graphophonic cues provide one source of information readers use to construct meaning from a text. For example, if students see a word like *date*, they use visual knowledge to identify letters, like *d* or *a*. They use sound knowledge to decide on possible sounds of the letters. They use phonics knowledge to connect visual and sound information. In this word, for instance, they use the silent *e* as a cue that the vowel sound in *date* is the long *a* sound.

As they read, children build up a knowledge of how graphophonics works. Any written language has limits on the possible combinations of letters and sounds that make up words. Readers build up their knowledge of these combinations and use this knowledge to confirm the predictions they make as they read. English speakers, for example, acquire the knowledge that, if the first letter of a word is *b* and a consonant follows, that the letter combinations could be *bl* or *br*, but never *bg*. They know that the *k* sound could be spelled with a *ck* at the end of a word, but never at the beginning.

Graphophonics, like the other cue systems, is more complex than many people realize. Students don't just connect the letter with its sound. Because of the complexity of the system, attempts at teaching it directly are likely to fail. Instead of learning graphophonics as the result of direct teaching, students acquire this knowledge as they read. Teachers still play an important role in helping students develop this cueing system. For a detailed account of how teachers working in meaning-centered classrooms do this, see Dahl et al. (1999). (See Chapter Eight for a discussion of the differences between phonics and graphophonics and the role of phonemic awareness in reading.)

Syntactic Cues

Good readers rely on more than letters and sounds, though. They also use their knowledge of how words go together. This is the syntax of the language. By using syntactic cues, readers can predict what kind of word will come next. For example, if a sentences begins "She put," students who are proficient in English will predict that the sentence will continue by telling *what* she put and *where* she put it. In English, we can't simply say, "She put the pen," and we can't say "She put on the table." On the other hand, if a sentence starts with "The big . . . " most readers would predict a noun like "boy" or "building" to follow. Proficient readers use their knowledge of syntactic patterns to make predictions about the kinds of words and phrases they will see in the rest of the sentence. Like graphophonics, though, syntax is too complex to be taught directly. Instead, students must acquire syntactic knowledge through transactions with texts.

Semantic Cues

The third cue system is semantics. Semantic cues aren't the same thing as the meaning of a text. There are three kinds of semantic cues. First, words and phrases themselves have meaning because they refer to things in the world. Children know that *chicken* refers to a barnyard animal. Words also have meanings that are not literal. *Chicken* can refer to a cowardly person. The literal and nonliteral meanings may not even be logically connected, and this poses real problems for English-language learners.

The second kind of semantic cue is the reader's knowledge of which words commonly go together. For example, in an article about baseball, a reader might predict other words like *batter, inning,* or *pitch.* Some words serve to connect parts of a text, and these words provide a third kind of semantic cue. For instance, *however* signals that what comes next contrasts with what went before. A pronoun like *she* usually refers to a name that occurred earlier. Readers use these cues to tie the parts of the text together.

These three kinds of semantic cues help readers make meaning as they read. By themselves, semantic cues do not constitute the meaning of the text.

Instead, they are one of the three sources of information in texts that readers can use, along with their background knowledge, to make sense of what they are reading. In the next section, we explain how readers use graphophonic, syntactic, and semantic cues as they read.

Strategies for Constructing Meaning

Readers use several strategies to construct meaning (Goodman, 1996). These strategies include sampling the text (looking at words and phrases), making predictions, making inferences (filling in missing information), confirming or disconfirming predictions, and integrating new knowledge. As readers use the strategies of sampling, predicting, inferring, confirming, and integrating, their focus is on making sense of the text. Below we explain each step in the process.

Sampling

The first step in reading is simply to look at the marks on the page. As they do this, readers "sample" the text. Beginning readers have to learn what to look at. At first, they may concentrate on the pictures rather than the text. They also have to decide where to look. Will the print be on the bottom of the page or at the top? It is difficult for young readers if the text on some pages is placed under the picture but on other pages over it. One of the characteristics of texts that support beginning readers is consistent placement of the print.

As readers become more proficient, they learn where to focus, and they begin to sample just enough text to get the graphophonic cues they need. They use these cues along with syntactic and semantic cues to construct meaning. They don't ignore the print cues, but neither do they focus on them too much. Effective sampling allows a reader to gather just enough information to make predictions.

Predicting

An important strategy in reading is predicting. Readers use their background knowledge and information from each of the cueing systems to make predictions. For example, readers use graphophonic cues to predict letter sequences. If a word begins with a consonant cluster such as *bl*, proficient readers predict that a vowel will follow.

Readers also use syntactic cues to make predictions. If a sentence starts,

"Bill persuaded," most readers would expect the next word to be the name of the person being persuaded. This would be followed by *to* and a verb. For example, the sentence might read, "Bill persuaded *Mary to go to the movies."*

At the same time, readers use semantic cues to guide their predictions. In the previous sentence, readers might predict that Bill would persuade Mary, but not that he would persuade a rock; and he might persuade her to go to the movies, but not to Pluto. Throughout this process, readers use their background knowledge to predict upcoming story events or topics.

English-language learners face a challenge in making predictions because they are still developing their English proficiency. They may not recognize common spelling patterns of English print, and they may not predict English syntactic patterns easily. However, if they concentrate on building meaning, they can predict upcoming story events. For that reason, reading instruction should focus on meaning-making rather than getting text details right. The more English-language learners read with a focus on meaning, the better they get at using all the cue systems because they are acquiring the academic language of texts.

Inferring

Writers never include all the possible information. Readers must fill in missing knowledge by making inferences. The writer might not describe the movie theater that Bill and Mary go to, for example, but readers can use their knowledge of movie theaters to infer these details. English-language learners can make certain kinds of inferences easily enough, but others may be more difficult. Writers might assume that readers will know about the physical setup and routine for attending an American movie, but some students may lack this information. Teachers can help students by building the background knowledge they will need to make inferences as they read.

Confirming or Disconfirming

When readers focus on meaning, they continually check to confirm their predictions. Is this word, phrase, sentence, paragraph, or text heading in the direction I thought it was? As long as the predictions are confirmed, proficient readers keep moving ahead, but when a prediction is disconfirmed, they go back to sample again and then correct. When teachers analyze students' reading using *miscue analysis*, they can see how well students confirm as they read. The term *miscue* comes from research by K. Goodman (1965). He defines a miscue as an unexpected response to a text. What that means is that when we listen to someone read and follow along, we expect the reader to say words that match the text. When the reader omits a word, inserts a word, substitutes one word for another, or reverses words, that is a miscue, because it is not what we expect. For example, Ann made the following miscue as she read:

Why shouldn't he whistle and jump over cracks in the sidewalk

and bound up the apartment house stairs ⟍ three at a time? the ⓒ

Ann substituted *the* for *three*. She predicted a different structure, and *the* didn't fit with what followed: "stairs the at a time" doesn't sound like English and doesn't make sense. Ann used the syntactic and semantic cues provided by the rest of the sentence to disconfirm her prediction. Since the miscue didn't make sense, she went back and corrected.

One procedure teachers have used to help students evaluate their own reading is *retrospective miscue analysis* (Goodman and Marek, 1996). Teachers tape-record students reading. Then, as they play back the tape, they pause at points where students make miscues and ask questions that help students check their sampling, predicting, and confirming. The questions relate to each of the cueing systems. For example, a teacher might ask:

♦ Does the miscue look (or sound) like what was on the page? (graphophonics)

♦ Does the miscue sound like language? (syntax)

♦ Does the miscue make sense? (semantics)

Often, teachers choose high-quality miscues to build up students' confidence. For example, if the student substitutes *house* for *home*, the answer to all three questions would be "Yes." This helps students understand that good readers don't always get the words right, but they do create sentences that make sense. Teachers may also choose some miscues that reflect an area in which students are consistently having trouble. One reader, for example, substituted *plan* for *plane* every time it appeared. The resulting sentences didn't make sense. The story tells of two brothers arguing, and the reader made this miscue:

plan!"
"You broke my *plane!"*

A teacher could play back the tape and ask whether "You broke my plan." makes sense. This would help the reader focus on constructing meaning during reading.

Integrating

As they continue through a text, readers continually integrate new information. They do this with cues from all three systems, and they do it at the level of word, phrase, sentence, and whole text. By keeping the focus on comprehension, they build up an understanding of what they are reading. When proficient readers have difficulty integrating new information, they make an adjustment. This might involve re-reading, reading on for more cues, or rethinking the ideas they have encountered.

Conclusion

Krashen's theory of language acquisition and the sociopsycholinguistic theory of literacy development provide the base for the Checklist of Effective Reading Instruction. Now that we have explained the theory base, we turn to the questions on the Checklist. In each of the chapters that follow, we show how teachers like Debbie and Veronica help all their students become proficient readers by following the guidelines provided by the Checklist.

Valuing Reading

Checklist Questions This Chapter Addresses

Question 1. Do students value themselves as readers, and do they value reading?
Question 2. Do students read frequently from a wide variety of genres?

Erin's Project

We begin by describing how one teacher found creative ways to help students value reading through reading a variety of texts:

> I went back to Carver Middle School (the site where I did my initial student teaching) and talked to some of the students about their attitudes toward reading and writing. Apathy toward reading and writing would be one way to describe the majority of the students' attitudes. The students were tired of the same old boring textbooks and writing assignments. It was a shock to me that these students didn't curl up on the couch on Saturday afternoons and read mystery novels, as I did when I was their age!

Erin, a middle school biology teacher, wrote this reflection as part of an inquiry project for a graduate class in language acquisition. Erin's goal was to "foster literacy" among six African American, Hispanic, and Southeast Asian eighth grade students who were struggling academically by working with them after school.

Erin began her work by having the students watch the movie *Bambi* together. They compared it with *The Lion King*, which they had seen on their own, and discussed different nature themes they noticed. She was interested that the Southeast Asian students (a Hmong student from Laos and a Cambodian student) as well as the African American and Hispanic students, drew on folklore from their own cultures that they shared. Together, the six students combined their ideas and wrote a short play. Erin was excited and encouraged by the students' response to this initial activity. She recorded some of their comments:

"I never knew I would actually like writing."
"Why can't teachers give homework like this?"
"I like the discussion. School is fun."

Since Erin knew she had both nonnative English speakers and reluctant readers in her group, she wanted to make reading as comprehensible and non-threatening as possible. She went to the library and picked out picture books that she thought would interest her students. She wanted them to begin to interact with texts and see how pictures can provide clues during reading. She read some stories aloud and encouraged students to tell their own stories through pictures. One Hmong boy reflected on this activity:

I always like to draw, but I don't know what this has to do with reading and writing. But then Miss English told me to make a story with just pictures. I kind of got what she meant. It was hard, but pictures tell all the story.

Next, Erin had the students listen to a tape about how different cultures explain occurrences in nature. Though the students snickered when "gods" were mentioned, the activity drew their interest, and they asked to create their own stories about why certain things happen in nature. Later, they shared these stories with each other.

As the students gained confidence and began to trust Erin more, they began to tell her about classroom assignments and academic struggles they were experiencing, including the upcoming U.S. Constitution test all eighth graders need to pass to graduate. Erin explained what happened next:

I asked the students if they had ever thought about reading books to prepare them to take the test, and they all grimaced when I mentioned the idea. The students and I went to the library downtown one day. Many students had never been to the library before and had to apply for their first library card. They chose a book to read about the Constitution. They were very surprised to find out that all books that deal with United States history do not look like textbooks. I was so happy to hear the students actually talk about books.

Going to the library gave Erin the opportunity to show the struggling older readers where to find picture books. She encouraged them to check these books out and read them to younger siblings. The students responded well to this and even brought Erin pictures and writing their brothers and sisters had drawn and written in response to their home tutoring sessions. The library visit and picture books were a real success. Erin reported her students' own words:

Cristina: "The visit to the library was fun. There are so many books for you to choose from."

Tascia: "I liked it, because I can read more books now, without having to buy them. I learned to pick out books that interested me."

Somchith: "I liked reading the children's books more than the others. They were much more exciting to look at and had more selection."

Through her after-school work with these students, Erin saw tremendous growth, not only in their reading and writing, but also in their confidence. As she so eloquently put it, "I hope I have opened the door just a bit wider. They no longer have to squeeze through. Different ways of helping students become literate are essential."

Erin helped her students value reading and value themselves as readers. She involved students in reading and discussing a variety of genres, and she helped her students enjoy reading and writing. Erin could certainly answer "yes" to the first two questions on the Checklist.

Joining the Literacy Club

Smith (1985) has developed a metaphor that describes what Erin did. He calls this involvement with reading "joining the literacy club." He explains that when students like Erin's "join the club," they "become members of a group of written language users" (124). Smith develops this metaphor by saying that when students become members of the club, it is understood that with time, they will become more experienced, but at first, they are not expected to be experts. He also points out that more experienced members of the club, like Erin, assume that some day new members will become as capable as they are. If students do not become members of the literacy club, it may be because they do not understand the benefits of literacy, or it may be that others, for one reason or another, expect that they will have trouble using written language. It is in "clubs" like this that students acquire literacy.

When Erin began to work with her students, they were not members of the club. They did not see that reading and writing had meaning and purpose. They did not believe that they could be members, because they believed it was too difficult. Because they were English-language learners or ethnic minorities, others may not have immediately expected them to become members of the club. However, once Erin helped these students to value reading and writing, they were ready to join the literacy club.

If we want students to join the literacy club, we must be sure that they see reading as the construction of meaning. When reading instruction focuses on decoding texts with little emphasis on the meaning or relevance of the texts, students become apathetic. They don't see how reading can serve a purpose for them. In order to value reading and to value themselves as readers, students must have the kinds of experiences Erin provided—experiences that engage them, make sense to them, and help them believe they can succeed.

Helping Students Value Reading and Value Themselves as Readers

Many teachers find ways to help students value reading and value themselves as readers. One way they do this is by reading books to students about reading and the importance of reading. For example, kindergarten and first grade students enjoy *Moonbear's Books* (Asch, 1997) and *I Like Books* (Browne, 1988), both of which promote the idea that it is enjoyable to read a lot of different books.

In Miriam Cohen's children's book, *When Will I Read?* (Cohen, 1977, 2–5), the kindergarten teacher helps her students value reading as she interacts with them daily. When Jim asks the teacher, "When will I read?" she tells him, "Soon." Jim persists with, "But when?" and she answers, "You know what the signs in our room say . . . 'You can read your name.'"

Jim responds, "But that's not really reading." The wise teacher smiles and says, "It will happen."

This teacher shows confidence that her students will become readers and provides the students with many opportunities to develop literacy:

♦ She fills the room with interesting books, reads to the students, and gives the children time to read.

♦ She involves them in a language-experience activity. When a garbage truck comes to collect the school trash, she takes the children out to watch. When they return to the classroom, she has them dictate what happened, and she writes their story on chart paper. Then, she reads the story back with the students. Jim remembers that one of the men on the truck asked, "How you doing, son?"

♦ She makes sure students have access to paper, pens, pencils, and markers, so they can do their own writing.

♦ Above all, the teacher is always ready to respond to students as they make discoveries about literacy. When Jim notices that the sign on the hamster cage has been torn and now reads, "Do let the hamsters out," he runs to tell the teacher. As she fixes the sign, she smiles at Jim and says, "I told you it would happen . . . You can read." Jim and the teacher put the new sign on the cage, and Jim concludes, "I've waited all my life . . . Now I can read."

Jim valued reading, in part because reading was so central to everything that went on in his kindergarten class. But he didn't see himself as a reader. Fortunately, his wise teacher supported Jim's literacy development, and by the end, Jim realized he could read. He then valued himself as a reader.

Valuing Primary-Language Literacy Development

Research shows that students literate in their first languages transfer that knowledge to English (Collier, 1995; Cummins, 1996; Krashen, 1996). Teachers need information about their students' primary-language literacy. Early in the school year, teachers can ask if their English learners have had schooling in their native countries or have learned to read in their native language in bilingual programs. Students who already know how to read will become proficient readers in English much more quickly than students who are learning English and also learning what reading is. This is true for older students as well as younger ones.

Janet, the same teacher whose quote opened our book, was amazed at how important information about the native language was in evaluating her students' progress in reading. When she began studying the importance of first-language literacy for her students, she reflected on the lack of comprehension in English reading she had noticed with her five Vietnamese students, even though they could read aloud quite well.

> At first I thought it was strange that these students could read every word of the material presented to them, but could not answer questions relating to the material they just read. Once I began to question these students about their knowledge of their native language, and discovered none of them could read or write in it, I saw a clear picture of why they had difficulty comprehending English.

In her own graduate studies, Janet had learned that the underlying process of reading in different languages is similar, even when the languages and writing systems appear to be different, and that literacy transfers across languages (Krashen, 1996). What followed was an important example of how teachers can value and support their students' first-language literacy as well as literacy in English. First, Janet decided to set up an after-school program for her Vietnamese students to help them learn to read and write in Vietnamese. She found a Vietnamese parent volunteer, provided space in her classroom for the tutoring sessions, and sent permission slips home explaining the plan home to parents. Parents were enthusiastic about the project. Janet described the results:

> The afternoon tutoring was a class of five Vietnamese students, who were excited about learning to read and write Vietnamese. The after-school tutoring sessions are a very special time for the students. They work one-on-one with the tutor and have a great time learning their native language.

In addition to promoting primary-language literacy, Janet used her primary-language tutor, a district-paid bilingual instructional aide, to help her students with English reading. Since her Vietnamese students were having trouble comprehending stories in English, Janet arranged for her tutor to discuss the stories with them in Vietnamese, both before and after they read them in class. After only three weeks, Janet could see results:

> [The students] are beginning to see that they understand the stories bet-
> ter after meeting with Ms. Thuy and going over the story content in
> Vietnamese. It has benefited the entire class, giving us the opportunity to
> have "whole class discussions" or "group discussion" about stories from
> the fourth grade reader. These students can engage in these discussions,
> and this has been a positive experience for English learners, for me, and
> for the entire class.

Janet and Erin took different approaches to helping their students
value reading and value themselves as readers. However, both teachers
knew their students' needs and interests, and both teachers built on what
the students already knew to help them become more proficient readers.
Both teachers also recognized the importance of connecting their students
with appropriate materials.

Reading Frequently from a Wide Variety of Genres

Reading is everywhere, and literate people must be able to read a wide variety of genres. The word *genre* simply means "kind" or "type." Students
need to be able to read many different kinds of texts in school. Figure 3–1
lists just a few of the genres students need to be able to read.

Literature	Expository Texts
▲ Fiction	▲ Content area texts
▲ Short stories	▲ Letters
▲ Novels	▲ Newspapers
▲ Poetry	▲ Magazine articles
▲ Drama	▲ Advertisements
▲ Nonfiction	▲ Messages
▲ Biographies	▲ Information pamphlets
▲ Autobiographies	▲ Instructions

Figure 3–1 Some Genres of Texts

Figure 3–1 divides texts into two general types: literature and expository texts. Literature includes both fiction and nonfiction. Fiction can be further broken down into principle types: short stories, novels, poetry, and plays. Of course, the list in Figure 3–1 is just a beginning. A genre like poetry could be subdivided into lyric, romantic, and so on.

To succeed in school, students need to be able to read these genres and more. A great deal of wonderful children's and adolescent literature is available for teachers to use to encourage their students to read for pleasure. However, students must also read from textbooks, newspapers, and magazines with their ads, charts, and graphs. In addition, they must be able to read and follow directions to websites, libraries on line, a variety of databases, and e-mail. Once on e-mail, they need to be able to maneuver through chat rooms or subscribe to listservs.

If, as we have argued, students acquire literacy when they engage with meaningful texts, then students must be exposed to different genres to acquire the ability to read those different kinds of texts. The principle here is the same as with acquiring language generally: While much of our knowledge of language can be generalized to different situations, some aspects of language are specific. If I am learning a second language, and I need to understand what a mechanic is telling me about the problems with my car, I need lots of comprehensible input related to cars.

In the same way, if students are going to read a particular genre, such as poetry, their general knowledge of reading will be very helpful. But to be a good reader of poetry, a student needs to read many different poems. Only by engaging with texts from this genre can students acquire the knowledge needed to read them proficiently.

As teachers plan their reading programs at any grade level, they should include different genres. Mary, a high school English and ESL teacher, requires both her mainstream English and her ESL students to compile a portfolio at the end of the year. In this portfolio, she asks her students to review their work for the year and include samples of six different papers or projects. Students write a one-page reflection for each item. Each portfolio includes the following papers or projects:

1. Something that reflects what you have learned this year
2. Something that shows your creativity
3. What you enjoyed working on the most
4. What was the most challenging assignment

5. How you integrated English with another subject
6. Two pieces or projects you compare and contrast

The portfolios that Mary's students assemble reflect the wide variety of genres her students read and write. Figure 3–2 shows the page René, an advanced ESL student, wrote about her most challenging assignment, her poetry book.

WAS THE MOST
CHALLENGING.

The most challenging work that I had done is the

"Poetry Book" because I had to go to the library, and chose

seven books about poems, and the ones that I chose were:

Love, Family, Death, Seasons, Friends, Animals and War.

I had to chose differents authors and differents books, and then

I had to go to computers room and type all my poems, and also

I had to made a bibliography to put the names of the books that

I chose and tha names of the authors, I spent to much time

because I translated some poems from Spanish.

Figure 3–2 René's writing

Characteristics of Texts

When teachers help students choose books, they need to consider two things: What genres do students need to be able to read to succeed, and what kinds of texts will support beginning and struggling readers? The two questions go hand in hand. Teachers can look at the genres their students need to be able to read and then choose texts from those genres that have characteristics that support reading. Figure 3–3 is a checklist teachers can use to decide whether or not a text has those characteristics (Freeman and Freeman, 1997).

Characteristics of Texts That Support Reading
1. Are the materials predictable? Prediction is based on the use of repetitive patterns, cumulative patterns, rhyme, alliteration, and rhythm.
2. Do the situations and characters in the book represent the experiences and backgrounds of the students in the class? Do the students have the necessary background for the concepts that are presented?
3. For picture books, do the visuals provide support for the text? Is the placement of the text and pictures predictable and easy to follow?
4. Are the materials interesting and/or imaginative?
5. Is the language in the texts natural? When there are only a few words on a page, do these limited-text books sound like real language, something people really say? If the book was translated, how good is the translation?

Figure 3–3 Checklist: Characteristics of Texts That Support Reading

Predictability

The first question on the Checklist asks whether the text is predictable. Making and confirming predictions is an important part of the meaning-centered theory of reading that we described in the last chapter. As Watson (1997, 636) explains, "Teachers realize that text itself, if it is predictable enough, helps children learn to read." Bialostok (1992), in a book for parents, talks about supporting children's reading through books that are predictable. Predictable books are important, because young readers can recognize patterns in the text, such as a refrain at the end of each section, or they can use features in the text like rhyme or rhythm. A good example of a predictable book is Mem Fox's (1997; 4, 6, 8) *Whoever You Are*. The author uses repeated patterns:

> Their skin may be
> different from yours,
> and their homes may be
> different from yours.
>
> Their schools may be
> different from yours,
> and their lands may be
> different from yours.

Fox not only uses the same syntactic pattern, she even breaks the lines at the same point. These features make the text highly predictable. This book also includes the refrain, "whoever they are, wherever they are, all over the world," to mark the end of each major section of the text.

Familiarity

Another feature that makes texts more predictable is familiarity. If students are familiar with the ideas, characters, and settings in a story or content text, they can make better predictions because they can anticipate what is likely to happen next in different situations. For teachers in multilingual classrooms, this is an important consideration. Often, English-language learners have different background experiences from mainstream students, so what may seem to be familiar settings, characters, and experiences for most students may be unfamiliar to students from other cultural backgrounds. On the other hand, some stories, such as fables, have been retold in different cultures, so all students may be familiar with them. For example, most students will know some version of a tale like "Cinderella." Teachers may want to bring in different versions to compare and contrast. This story is predictable, because most students will be familiar with the characters and events.

Krashen (1985) has shown the benefits of having students read a number of books by the same author. He calls this "narrow reading." Why is this kind of reading good? If you have read a series of books by a favorite writer, you know the answer. Certain patterns emerge. The same kinds of characters have similar experiences from book to book. When Yvonne began her fourth book in the Mitford series (Karon, 1999), for example, she knew it would be about Father Tim, she knew the setting would be in a small town in the south, and she even knew the kinds of language to expect. All this familiar information made the book more predictable. Because a book is more predictable, it provides more comprehensible input, and students acquire more aspects of literacy.

Prediction plays an important role in reading. Readers construct meaning by making and confirming predictions, using background knowledge and information from the three cueing systems. Whether or not a text is predictable, then, depends on both the features of the text and the experience of the readers. Readers can more easily make predictions if texts follow obvious patterns and if the topics are those that student's have experience with and interest in. Teachers can only determine predictability if they know the text and also know their students. Then their job becomes one of connecting their students with the right texts. That's what Erin did so well. (See Chapter Eight, for a discussion of how predictability differs from readability formulas and decodable texts.)

Other Characteristics of Texts That Support Reading

Visuals

Illustrations, pictures, charts, and graphs provide nonlinguistic context cues that help students make sense of text. Erin, for example, was aware that she should choose books that offered additional support from illustrations for the struggling older readers she worked with. Visuals are helpful if they match the text well. Some books have beautiful illustrations, but the pictures do not offer clues for key vocabulary in the text. In addition, texts are easier to read if the visuals are on the same page or the same two-page spread as the text the pictures refer to. Similarly, books are easier to read if the words are placed consistently from page to page. Some books for young readers are actually quite difficult, even for adults to read aloud, because on one page the words are under the picture and on the next page the words are placed over the illustration.

Interesting, Imaginative Texts

If one goal of reading is to help students value reading, it is crucial to connect them with interesting and imaginative texts. A wonderful example of such a text is *If . . .* (Perry, 1995). Each page has a beautiful illustration and a brief text that follows the pattern "If __ were ____ . . ." For example, one page shows a girl smiling, and the text reads: "If toes were teeth . . ." When students look closely, they see that the girl's mouth is full of toes! Other pages include: "If dogs were mountains . . ." and "If frogs ate rainbows . . ." Imaginative texts like this one draw students into reading and also lend themselves to art projects and writing assignments.

Yvonne read the first pages of *If . . .* to her graduate students—all teachers studying language acquisition. Then she showed them other pages and asked them what they thought the text might read based on the illustrations. Once students understood the model, she had them work in groups to make up original drawings and text pages. Each group wrote the text on one side of a piece of butcher paper and their illustration on the other side. Then, they held up the pictures for classmates to guess the text. One of Yvonne's favorites was the group that illustrated "If flowers could blow kisses." The group completed their illustration by applying fresh lipstick, puckering up, and kissing the paper. After doing this activity, many of the teachers in Yvonne's class used this imaginative text in their own classrooms.

Natural Language

Texts support reading if the language is natural. Natural texts are also more predictable, because they follow familiar patterns. When writing limited-text books for beginning readers, authors face a real challenge to create stories with only a few words on each page and still include natural-sounding language. Some authors have succeeded in creating interesting, natural-sounding language in books with only a few words per page. Often, they do this by spreading a sentence over several pages. Ann Morris has written a number of very simple books that have only a few words on each page. For example, her book *Bread, Bread, Bread* has only a few words on each page:

p. 7   People eat bread all over the world.

p. 8   There are many kinds, many shapes, many sizes—

p. 9   skinny bread, fat bread, round flat bread, bread with a hole,

p. 10 crunchy bread, lunchy bread . . .

p. 11 and bread to soak up your egg.

This book and others by Morris are excellent for struggling older readers for a number of reasons:

♦ They are authentic. They were written to inform, not to teach a grammar point or a sound-spelling pattern.

♦ The texts are limited. There are only a few words on each page.

♦ There is a good text-picture match that provides the nonlinguistic context readers need to make sense of the text.

♦ The photographs make the books more appealing to older students, who sometimes reject limited-text books with pictures designed for young children.

♦ The text provides opportunities to focus on sounds and spellings (e.g., crunchy bread, lunchy bread).

♦ The books have a multicultural perspective, with photographs from around the world.

Many of the Morris books have been translated. When possible, teachers using these translations should check to see if they also contain natural language. The Morris books have many of the characteristics that support reading. Figure 3–4 lists several of these books.

Bread, Bread, Bread. New York: Mulberry Books. (1989).

Hats, Hats, Hats. New York: Lothrop, Lee & Shepard Books. (1989).

Con cariño. Carmel, Calif.: Hampton Brown. (1990).

Loving. New York: William Morrow. (1990).

Sombreros, gorras y cachucas. New York: Scholastic. (1991).

Houses and Homes. New York: Lothrop, Lee and Shepard Books. (1992).

Shoes, Shoes, Shoes. Carmel, Calif.: Hampton-Brown Books. (1995).

Weddings. New York: Lothrop, Lee and Shepard Books. (1995)

On the Go. Boston: Houghton Mifflin. (1996).

Figure 3–4 Ann Morris Bibliography

Teachers who follow effective practices know that an important part of their job is to find the right texts for their students. Teachers can use the Checklist we have provided (Figure 3–3) to select texts that support reading. Such texts provide the comprehensible input students need to acquire literacy. We conclude this chapter with another example of an effective teacher who connected his students with appropriate texts from a variety of genres, so that they could value reading and value themselves as readers.

Effective Reading Instruction Through a "Life in the Ocean" Unit

We introduced Francisco in the Introduction as a credentialed Spanish/ English bilingual teacher now teaching in a coastal setting where English Only is the district policy in the aftermath of the California English Only Initiative. Previously, he taught a bilingual second and third grade class in a rural town in the Central Valley of California. Below, we describe an ocean unit Francisco has taught each year. First, we describe what Francisco did when he was in a bilingual classroom, and then we explain the adaptations he made in the more-restrictive, English Only setting. In both settings, Francisco demonstrates how important it is for his students to read and be exposed to a variety of different genres.

The Ocean Unit in a Bilingual Setting

At the rural school in his second and third grade multiage bilingual classroom, Francisco taught students who were all native Spanish speakers. Most of his migrant students were in his class because they were identified by other teachers as struggling in school. Like Janet with her Vietnamese students, Francisco knew that literacy and content knowledge developed in the first language transfers to the second language (Cummins, 1981), and that once his students could read, write, and learn academic content in their native language, they would be able to use English more confidently for academic purposes.

Francisco organized around themes because he understood that that type of organization supported his students' language acquisition and concept development. A key strategy he used was "preview/view/review" (see Figure 3–5). This proven strategy works well for both teachers of bilingual students and teachers with a few English learners in their classrooms (Freeman and Freeman, 1998).

Francisco implemented preview/view/review using a wide variety of

Preview	First Language	The teacher gives an overview of the lesson or activity in the students' first languages (this could be done by giving an oral summary, reading a book, showing a film, asking a key question' etc.).
View	Second or Target Language [English]	The teacher teaches the lesson or directs the activity in the students' second language.
Review	First Language	The teacher or the students summarize key ideas and raise questions about the lesson in their first languages.

Figure 3–5 Preview/View/Review

literature and content texts. Because his students came from a rural, agricultural area and most had had little previous experience with the sea, Francisco wanted to start his unit by giving them time to think about and talk about the ocean and its inhabitants. The activities he planned served as a primary language preview.

He read them two limited text books, *Un cuento curioso de colores* (*A Fish Color Story*) (Wylie and Wylie, 1983) and *Un cuento de peces y sus formas* (*A Fishy Shape Story*) (Wylie and Wylie, 1985), to give them ideas about the colors and forms of fish in the sea. Francisco then invited students to use their imaginations to make their own fish, using different colors and shapes. As they worked, students chatted informally in Spanish and English about their fish creations and what they knew about the fish. The finished projects were then put on the wall to form a multicolored fish kaleidoscope quilt. The next day, Francisco read the English version of the two Wylie and Wylie books, as well as *Fish Eyes: A Book You Can Count On* (Ehlert, 1990), a colorful counting book showing shapes and designs on fish. Since the students had heard two of the stories in Spanish and had made their own fish as a preview, the English stories were more comprehensible.

The next day, Francisco continued with the preview activities by reading the students a big book content book, *En aguas profundas* (*In the Depths*) (García-Moliner, 1993). After a short discussion of the reading, Francisco wrote on the whiteboard, "Qué sabemos del mar?" (What do we know about the sea?) Students responded in Spanish by telling him about the water in the ocean, shells on the beach, the names of some fish, and some personal experiences. Then Francisco wrote, "Qué quieren saber del mar?" (What do you want to know about the sea?) This question led students to ask questions about different sea animals, especially "delfines" (dolphins), "ballenas" (whales), and "tiburones" (sharks).

The discussion and brainstorming in Spanish served as the preview for instruction in English (the "view" portion of the plan). Francisco began with a picture walk through the book, *The Mighty Ocean* (Berger, 1996), a book that paralleled the content of *En aguas profundas*. For the picture walk, Francisco asked students to look at the pictures in the big book and comment to each other quietly on what they saw. He also asked them what things they saw there that they could talk about in English. Once they finished looking at the book, students shared English words and phrases about the ocean from the book and Francisco wrote them on a piece of butcher paper. Then Francisco read the book to them, stopping to answer their questions and to discuss parts that especially caught their interest.

Next, Francisco read the big book, *Fishy Facts* (Chermayeff, 1997). He followed this reading by having the students meet in small groups to discuss what facts they had learned. Students could go back to the book and use their primary language as they reviewed the main ideas. He then led the students through a brainstorm session in English of all the facts that they found in the book about fish.

In the days that followed, Francisco and his students read many more stories, poems, content books, and magazines in Spanish and English on the topic of the ocean. Francisco's students also wrote stories in English and Spanish about the ocean. Their writing reflected their acquisition of both Spanish and English and their ability to use different genres. For example, Veronica wrote and illustrated an eight-page story in Spanish, entitled El pez feliz (The Happy Fish)," which was similar to the story, "El pez arcoiris" (Pfister, 1994) that Francisco had read in class. Juan and Jackie wrote stories in English, entitled "The Dolphins Jumping" and "Dolphins Flipper," which showed what they had learned by reading content books about dolphins. Other students wrote poems modeled on the poems they had read together in class.

After learning so much about the ocean, the students engaged in several culminating activities. They talked about posters that Francisco brought in. The posters, entitled "Fish that We Eat," "Fish that Eat Us," "Shells, Shellfish," and "Man Abuses the Sea," were put in one corner of the room for students to refer to during writing and discussions. Each student created a poster about the ocean in English. The students could choose to draw and write anything they wanted on the posters, but most students chose to write about taking care of the ocean. The walls of Francisco's room were covered with posters, including "Save the Whales," "Don't Throw Garbage in the Ocean," "We Need to Take Care of the Ocean or We Are Going to Die," and "Save the Ocean. It's the Home of the Fish."

The culminating activity was the creation of a huge mural of the sea and the seacoast. In groups of four, the children chose animals and plants they had learned about. They looked at the posters and looked through various books to gather information. Using construction paper, they made different sea animals and plants. Then the class worked together to place their creations on the mural. Finally, the students dictated to Francisco in English a description of their mural, which was typed on the computer, printed in large letters, and placed next to the mural.

The Ocean Unit in an English Only Setting

When Francisco moved to a small city on the coast with a high Hispanic population, he was hired to teach in a school district that adopted an English Only policy. This change worried Francisco, who had studied the rationale for bilingual education and the research that showed that prolonged first language support leads to long-term academic success (Collier and Thomas, 1996; Krashen, 1996; Krashen, 1999). Two factors, however, forced Francisco to make changes in his use of Spanish in the classroom. The administration insisted he use English for the majority of his instruction, and he now had native English speakers as well as native Spanish speakers in his class.

Francisco found that he still used preview/view/review. However, he used far more English texts and limited the Spanish preview to some of his personal books and some brief introductions to topics. He also allowed students to ask him questions in Spanish during the review time if they were unclear about concepts or vocabulary. While he used less Spanish in class, he encouraged students to continue to read and write Spanish at home and consistently validated the importance of their language and culture.

Francisco followed many of the same activities he used before with his bilingual students in this ocean theme, but he needed to find additional comprehensible and engaging texts in English to be sure his students were developing concepts and vocabulary in English. Many of the additional books he found came from a collection of high-interest content and literature books put together to support older readers in the "Soar to Success " program (Cooper, 1999).

Francisco connected the new books to readings and activities he had done in the past. For example, after reading *The Ocean Alphabet Book* (Pallotta, 1986), he invited students to add to the brainstormed list of facts about fish and the ocean that the students had already begun with the *Fishy Facts* book. Since whales, dolphins, and sharks also fascinated his students living on the coast, he searched for and found more fact books about those animals, including *Whales* (Simon, 1999), *Whales* (DuTemple, 1999), *Baby Whales Drink Milk* (Esbensen, 1999), *Whales and Dolphins* (Sabin, 1985), and *Sharks* (McGovern, 1976). He also found other colorful information books, including *Coral Reef Hunters* (Ethan and Bearanger, 1999), *Sea Turtles* (Staub, 1999), and a resource book with all kinds of ocean facts, *The Kingfisher Young People's Book of Oceans* (Lambert, 1999).

Since Francisco's new students lived near the ocean, they had an even greater desire to be sure that the ocean and its animals were preserved. To begin discussion on the use and abuse of water and water animals, Francisco read his students *Water* (Asch, 1995), a limited-text book that starts students thinking about conservation issues. He connected this book to a true story, *The Story of Three Whales* (Whittell, 1999), about an Alaskan community that labored hard to save three whales trapped under the ice. Other stories Francisco read and discussed with his students about the abuse of oceans and ocean animals were *Why Are the Whales Vanishing?* (Asimov, 1999), *Oil Spill!* (Berger, 1999), and *Antarctica* (Cowcher, 1999).

Figure 3–6 lists the books that Francisco used during this unit.

Aliki. 1993. "El celacanto perdido." *In En aguas profundas*. Boston: Houghton Mifflin.

Barrett, N. 1991. *Ballenas*. New York: Franklin Watts.

———. 1991. *Delfines*. New York: Franklin Watts.

———. 1991. *Tiburones*. New York: Franklin Watts.

Berger, M. 1996. *The Mighty Ocean*. New York: Newbridge Communications Inc.

Bracho, C. 1993. *Jardín del mar, Reloj de versos*. México, D.F.: CIDCLI.

Chermayeff, I. 1997. *Fishy Facts, Invitaciones*. Boston: Houghton Mifflin.

Cowcher, H. 1999. *Antarctica*. Boston: Houghton Mifflin.

Craig, J. 1987. *Cómo son los habitantes del mar, Cómo son*. México, D.F.: SITESA.

DeSaix, F. 1991. *The Girl Who Danced With the Dolphins*. New York: Farrar, Straus and Giroux.

Dubovoy, S. 1990. *Poncho, el cangrejo presumido*. México, D.F.: SITESA.

———. 1991. *Turquesita, Colección Barril Sin Fondo*. Amecameca: C.E.L.T.A.

Ehlert, L. 1990. *Fish Eyes: A Book You Can Count On*. New York: Trumpet.

Fernández, F. (Traductora). 1984. *A la orilla del mar, Biblioteca temática para niños: Coleccion naturaleza*. México, D. F.: Fernández Editores.

García-Moliner, G. 1993. *En aguas profundas, Celebremos la literatura*. Boston: Houghton Mifflin.

Garland, P. 1992. *La orilla del mar*. Crystal Lake, Ill.: Rigby.

Girón, N. 1993. *El mar, Celebremos la literatura*. Boston: Houghton Mifflin.

Granrows, A. 1986. *La ballena azul*. Lexington, Mass.: Schoolhouse Press.

Kovacs, D. 1987. *A Day Under Water*. New York: Scholastic.

Lauber, P. 1996. "An Octopus is Amazing." In *Treasure*. Boston: Houghton Mifflin.

Pallotta, J. 1986. *The Ocean Alphabet Book*. New York: Trumpet

Pfister, M. 1994. *El pez arco iris*. New York: Ediciones Norte-Sur.

Revello, R. 1996. "Las canciones de mi isla." *In Observa la naturaleza*. Boston: Houghton Mifflin.

Sands, S. 1997. "Oceans." New York: *Kids Discover*.

Sheldon, D. 1993. *El canto de las ballenas*. Translated by Nelson Rivera. Caracas, Venezuela: Ediciones Ekaré.

Wilson, L. 1991. *El mar y la costa. Educación ambiental*, ed. Rodolfo Fonseca. México, D.F.: CONAFE.

Wylie, J. and D. Wylie. 1983. *Un cuento curioso de colores*. New York: Childrens Press.

———. 1985. *Un cuento de peces y sus formas*. New York: Childrens Press.

Zoehfeld, K. 1994. *Dolphin's First Day*. New York: Scholastic.

———. "¿Qué vive en una concha?" In *Invitaciones*. Boston: Houghton Mifflin.

———. 1996. "What lives in a shell?" In *Friends*. Boston: Houghton Mifflin.

Figure 3–6 Ocean Unit Bibliography

Students in Francisco's classes learned a great deal during their study of the ocean. By organizing his curriculum around a theme and using the preview/view/review method along with a variety of high-interest books and interactive strategies, Francisco helped his students develop important content knowledge. By the end of this extended unit, Francisco's students confidently read many texts representing different genres. In this process, they were learning to value reading and to value themselves as readers.

Supporting 4 Reading

Checklist Questions This Chapter Addresses

Question 3. Do students see teachers engaged in reading for pleasure as well as for information?
Question 4. Do students have a wide variety of reading materials to choose from and time to read?
Question 5. Do students make good choices for their reading?

Mary's Class

Mary, the high school teacher we described in the Introduction, has established a routine to engage all her students in meaningful reading.

The first bell rings, and the high school students begin to wander into their classrooms. Some are laughing and teasing each other. One student, Mario, pushes another playfully. Mary, his teacher, who is reading a novel at her desk, looks up at the student, shakes her head, and then continues to read. Mario shrugs and then walks over to the bookshelf where he picks up a paperback of short stories, *Baseball in April and Other Stories* (Soto, 1990) written by a local author the class has talked about and read before, Gary Soto. Other students pull books out of their backpacks or pick up paperbacks or magazines from the bookshelf. By the time the second bell rings, students are in their seats and beginning to read. Two ESL students are pointing to pictures and commenting quietly on a copy of *Sports Illustrated* that features their favorite basketball team. It takes about five minutes for everyone to settle into the daily fifteen-minute reading time, but once they all do, the room is quiet, with everyone, including the teacher, engrossed in their reading.

The high school where Mary teaches has a large Hispanic population, as well as a sizable group of students whose first language is Punjabi. Students in Mary's English classes follow a typical routine each day (Freeman and Freeman, 1998). Mary has found that this is especially important for her ninth graders, who are often intimidated by high school and its schedules and demands. Of course, this kind of routine is also helpful to English-language learners, as they are able to predict what is expected of them during class. The routine allows these students to spend their energies in making sense of the curriculum, instead of worrying about what they are supposed to be doing.

Mary was reading a book as the students came into the room. She continued to read, despite the slightly chaotic nature of the first minutes of class, and the students eventually settled down to read as well. Although this routine had to be established at the beginning of the year, Mary's reading demonstrated that this was reading time, and that reading was something their teacher valued and expected her students to value, too. As a result, she can answer "yes" to the third question on the Checklist for Effective Reading Instruction.

Mary's students see their teacher engaged in reading for pleasure as well as for information. Mary reads because, like Erin, she wants her students to become members of the literacy club. Smith (1983) identifies three steps that are necessary for joining the club. They include demonstrations, engagement, and sensitivity.

Demonstrations

Smith's definition of *demonstrations* is not the traditional one we think of, in which a teacher models specific steps to show students how to do something. According to Smith, we provide a demonstration whenever we do something we think is important and others observe us. For example, children may watch adolescents practicing basketball shots for hours on end. They are receiving demonstrations of how to play basketball, and they are also receiving demonstrations that playing basketball is a worthwhile activity. As a result, they develop the desire to participate themselves. We may not even be aware we are providing a demonstration. Parents sometimes only become aware of the demonstrations they have given when they observe certain behaviors in their own children (usually when someone is visiting). But demonstrations can also be planned, and that's what Mary does when she reads at the beginning of each class.

Demonstrations help students learn how to perform certain activities, but they can also help students develop certain attitudes. When children see their parents reading the morning paper, they receive a demonstration that reading, specifically reading the morning paper, is an important and valuable thing to do. When adults not only read, but then share information they find in the newspaper, children are given a demonstration of how people talk about texts. If younger siblings see older brothers and sisters curled up with a good book, they get a demonstration of how pleasurable reading can be.

Engagements

Demonstrations show people how to do things, and they show them that some things are worth doing. The next step is engagement in the activity. Even very young children can be seen sitting on a couch with an open book. They are "reading" the book, imitating other family members and sometimes using memorized words picked up from being read to. This kind of engagement is an important early step in learning to read.

In schools, teachers often have trouble getting students to engage in reading, especially students who do not value reading or value themselves as readers. Teachers use different strategies, as Erin did, to engage students, including using high-interest materials, previewing the materials, and making sure the reading has a purpose for the students. In her class, Mary allowed the ESL students to work in pairs to read a high-interest magazine. This collaborative reading helped her students to engage with the text. No learning can take place without engagement.

Sensitivity

The third step in learning something is sensitivity. Smith (1983, 105) defines sensitivity as "the absence of any expectation that learning will not take place or that it will be difficult." The kindergarten teacher in *When Will I Read?* (Cohen, 1977) certainly showed sensitivity when she assured Jim he would learn to read by telling him with confidence: "It will happen." Parents and teachers seldom doubt that their children will learn to walk or talk. They never do or say things that suggest walking and talking will be difficult. Children and older students learn to read if they have demonstrations of others reading, if they engage in reading, and if parents and teachers never show a doubt that they will read.

A wonderful example of parents who show sensitivity comes from the children's story, *Leo the Late Bloomer* (Krauss, 1971). Leo, a young tiger, can't do anything right. He can't read, write, draw, or even talk. Leo's father is concerned, but his mother assures the father that "Leo is just a late bloomer." Leo's father isn't convinced. Every day, he watches Leo for "signs of blooming," and finally he asks: "Are you sure Leo's a bloomer?" The wise mother replies: "Patience . . . . A watched bloomer doesn't bloom." So Leo's father watches TV instead of Leo. He waits and waits until one day, "in his own good time, Leo bloomed!" Leo's parents (and especially his mother) never show Leo that they doubt he will someday read and write, draw and talk like other young tigers. Their patience is rewarded when one day Leo begins to read, write, draw, and speak beautifully. Their sensitivity promoted Leo's learning.

Sensitivity is an important part of learning to read, but parents are bombarded with messages that may cause them to doubt that their children will succeed. The daily news declares the dismal state of reading in this country, despite the fact that a careful look at NAEP (National Assessment of Educational Progress) scores shows that from the first year NAEP was administered to 1996, "reading achievement has either stayed even or increased slightly" (McQuillan, 1998, 2). In the most recent international reading tests, the nine-year-old children in the United States ranked second only to Finland, and the fourteen-year-olds placed "a very respectable 9th out of 31" (8). McQuillan points out that even that score of ninth "is somewhat deceiving, since the United States was virtually tied with 5 other countries after fourth-place New Zealand" (9). Analyses like those carried out by McQuillan and others (Berliner and Biddle, 1995; Krashen, 1996; Krashen, 1999) should be widely publicized to create a positive atmosphere in which parents and school officials come to believe that all students can develop high levels of literacy.

Building a Classroom Library

In Mary's class, students are given demonstrations of the importance of reading, and Mary always shows confidence that all her students will read. However, many of her students can only engage in reading because she has built up her classroom library.

Each period begins with fifteen minutes of SSR (Sustained Silent Reading). If students do not bring their own books or books from the school library, Mary has them choose from her classroom library of about 250 books, which includes short stories, poetry, and novels at different levels of complexity. Besides traditional works, Mary makes certain her library also has some short, fairly easy, predictable texts, including "choose your own adventure" books, books from the Goosebumps series (Stine), and teen romances such as *Sweet Valley High* (Pascal).

Mary makes a special effort to include in her library works by Latino and Latina writers. For example, she has found that books by Gary Soto, such as *Buried Onions, Baseball in April: And Other Stories, Crazy Weekend, Living up the Street,* and *Neighborhood Odes* (Soto, 1990, 1997, 1994, 1992, 1996) are especially relevant to her students, because Soto writes about everyday experiences of Hispanics in nearby Fresno and environs. An especially helpful resource for locating relevant books is *Latino and Latina Voices in Literature* (Day, 1997). For students who are intimidated by reading in English, Mary also has some books in Spanish, because she knows that reading proficiency developed in one language transfers to another. This wide variety of reading materials ensures that all students are reading something daily.

Since her classroom is filled with books, Mary can answer "yes" to question four on the Checklist for Effective Reading Instruction. Her students do have a wide variety of reading materials to choose from and time to read. Often, it is only through the efforts of individual teachers like Mary that all students have access to books.

Mike's Classroom Library

In many schools with limited school libraries, teachers have sacrificed to build classroom libraries. Mike, who teaches fourth grade students in an inner city school, describes the extensive classroom library he has set up to meet the needs and interests of his students. He includes a wide variety of genres, so that his students have exposure to different reading experiences:

> The classroom is full of a wide range of reading materials, that serve to support the connection between the reading and writing processes. Within the classroom are over two thousand titles from a general library collection; multiple-copy text sets; a set of resource books, including encyclopedias, a thesaurus, dictionaries, atlases, and telephone directories; a great number and variety of periodicals; a modest collection of second language titles, mostly Spanish, with a few in Hmong, Vietnamese, and Cambodian. There is also a large collection of student-published

works, representing past students' writing as well as current work. An additional collection of current student-published works is available in a special student-created rack in the school library.

Many other teachers, like Mike and Mary, have made special efforts, so that their students have access to books and time to read. They know, and the research shows, that access to good books is essential for the acquisition of literacy. Quite simply, students won't value reading if they don't have appropriate books to read. Often schools and communities lack good libraries, and teachers have to find ways to gather the books themselves. They make these extra efforts, because they are convinced that a good reading program begins with good books.

Yvonne has surveyed teachers to find how they have built their classroom libraries over time. The following represents a composite list of suggestions from knowledgeable educators:

◆ Use bonus points from different book clubs, such as Troll and Scholastic.

◆ Go to garage sales.

◆ Watch for yearly library sales of old books.

◆ Note publisher warehouse special sales in larger cities.

◆ Put notices in church and club bulletins and newsletters asking for donations of children's books from personal home collections.

◆ Ask retiring teachers for books they will no longer use.

◆ Solicit donations from local service clubs.

◆ Ask businesses to donate books or money to buy books.

◆ Organize a moneymaking project in the classroom for purchase of books.

◆ Turn in book order requests frequently to administrators. There is sometimes money that needs to be spent quickly.

◆ Watch for grant money available through professional organizations, and write a short proposal to increase your classroom library.

◆ Write publishing companies, including textbook companies, and ask them to donate books.

Building a School Library

Many school districts have implemented programs that include all the elements necessary for students to join the literacy club. Ann, a Title I reading specialist in Nogales, Arizona, developed one such program. Ann works at a bilingual charter school that specializes in meeting the personal, cultural, and academic needs of the children and the community.

One of the reasons the charter school was established was that the children in this low-income area were not succeeding academically. Very few children were reading at grade level in either Spanish or English, according to standardized tests. Before the charter school was set up, many of the children in the community had very little access to books. Ann and her coworkers knew that many families had few books in the home, and they were convinced that getting books into the hands of the students would make a difference for them academically. Ann's first challenge in creating an effective reading program was to build up the school library.

Ann has been able to build an excellent library for this small charter school, which is housed in some large, older homes in the inner city. The library has been set up in one home, in a pleasant room with cozy corners that invite reading. With the help of some of the older students, Ann went through all the unorganized boxes of books the school had and arranged them on shelves around the room. As she set up the library, Ann found quite a few interesting and attractive books that were not being used, because no one had had a chance to organize or display them. She also found several sets of limited-text, predictable books that would support beginning readers in Spanish and English.

With some grant money, Ann ordered predictable big books in Spanish and English, as well as quite a few high-quality hardback children's literature and content books. Before making the orders, she consulted colleagues who specialized in children's literature in Spanish and English so that she would have a good selection of materials for readers of different ages and interests. In addition to buying books, Ann contacted some textbook companies whose reading programs include quality children's literature and asked for sample materials for the school library. She was pleased with the response and soon found her biggest problem was to organize a computerized library loan system to keep track of all the books.

Ann's Literacy Club

Ann realized that making books available was just a first step. In addition to gathering and organizing books, she started a cross-age tutoring program called The Literacy Club. She read about other programs that had operated successfully in multilingual contexts (Samway, 1995). Ann knew that her program should give younger students demonstrations of the importance of reading and opportunities to engage with interesting reading materials, as they participated in sessions with older readers. Reading with younger students gave the older readers, in turn, opportunities to read rich literature to and with others.

An important part of The Literacy Club program was the training Ann provides for the tutors. Ann knew that it was important for the older students who act as tutors to take a positive attitude and exhibit a clear belief that all the younger students would become proficient readers.

Before the first session, the teens were asked to make a Literacy Timeline, featuring the highs and lows of their personal reading history. At the first session, they shared their timelines in small groups. Then, the whole group used this information to develop a list of good and bad reading experiences they had had. Ann typed the list up and used it during the second session to emphasize the importance of giving the young readers positive experiences. She also reminded the tutors to avoid activities that they listed among their own bad experiences, such as "reading in front of the class" and "listening to others read stories without expression."

Once the tutors shared their own reading experiences, Ann engaged them in activities to help them understand key concepts and strategies involved in reading. These included:

Choosing Books

Ann read a book to the tutors and discussed with them what makes some texts easy and others hard. She used the Checklist: Characteristics of Texts that Support Reading (Figure 3–3) as a guide. She showed students examples of books that meet the Checklist criteria, including predictable books and limited-text books with natural language. Then, she put a variety of books on a table and had the students work together to evaluate each one, using the Checklist.

Planning the Sessions

Ann also helped the tutors plan their sessions for this after-school program, which runs one and one half hours each day Monday through Thursday. Planning involves deciding who is going to read, what they will read, and what they will talk about before, during, and after reading the books. She included discussion of how tutors might respond when children have trouble during the reading. She encouraged them to keep the focus on meaning. She pointed out that if they correct every mistake or supply a word when the child pauses that the child will not become an independent reader. She told them that they should help the child use the context to figure out difficult passages, rather than trying to sound each word out.

Implementing Strategies

In her training sessions, Ann demonstrated specific strategies the tutors can use during the sessions. Then she had the students practice with one another. She knew these strategies would help the tutors, as well as the younger students. Some of the strategies include:

♦ Read-Alouds—Ann showed the tutors how read a big book to a group of young students. She demonstrated how to hold the book and how to get a student to help turn the pages. She also explained how she gathered the children on the rug in front of her and had the youngsters sit cross-legged.

♦ Partner Reading—Ann discussed different ways the tutors can interact once they start working in pairs. They could first read to the child. Ann showed the tutors how to track the print as they read, by running their finger under each line. She pointed out that the children can later begin to do the tracking. She also demonstrated how to read with the children, using a technique called Echo Reading. In Echo Reading, the two start out reading together. If the younger reader is fairly confident, the older reader fades out. The tutor comes back in and reads again at points where the child is struggling. Once the child begins to read more confidently, the tutor again fades out. If the younger reader is less confident from the beginning, the tutor does more of the reading and encourages the child to chime in on those parts she can read, and to read along as much as possible.

♦ Picture Walk—Ann showed the tutors how they could present a picture book to a young reader. They could "walk" through the book, showing each picture and asking the children to tell what they see and what they think is happening. This is a good strategy, especially for English-language learners, to provide needed vocabulary and to assess the background knowledge the child brings to the reading. (See Chapter Eight for a discussion of the problems of trying to teach vocabulary directly.)

Besides these general strategies for approaching reading, Ann suggests some specific techniques to the tutors.

♦ Stop the reading occasionally, and ask the child to predict what might come next.

♦ Act out the story.

♦ Break the story into parts to discuss, or discuss the whole story at the end.

♦ Avoid typical comprehension questions, and instead, use more general questions, such as those developed by Hansen (1989): What do you remember? What else would you like to know? What does this story remind you of? These questions focus on making sense of texts and connecting them to the reader's life.

♦ Have the child write about the story. The child can draw pictures and label them, sequencing the story by drawing pictures that represent the beginning, middle, and end of the story. Children use the labeled pictures to retell the story

♦ Use Language Experience. Ask the child to retell the story, and write down what the child says. Read back the child's story together.

The charter school where Ann works is located in a poor community, so creating an accessible library was a high priority, and the Literacy Club was established to make sure that there were specific times set aside for students to read. The library is well-supplied with books in both Spanish and English, and the bilingual tutors read and talk about books with students in both languages.

The Importance of Access to Books

Ann built a good school library to ensure that students had access to books. She also trained the tutors so they could provide demonstrations of reading and engage the students in meaningful reading activities. These same components are key elements of a series of large-scale programs initiated by Warwick Elley, who has studied literacy development throughout the world. Students in Elley's programs made significant gains in vocabulary simply by being read to. He also reports sharp gains in knowledge of English grammar. (See Chapter Eight for a discussion of teaching vocabulary directly.)

Elley has found that children trying to learn to read English, especially those from third world countries, lack resources, qualified teachers, and exposure to English. His research on literacy development with young children all over the world in places like Fiji, Singapore, Sri Lanka, and South Africa (Elley, 1991, 1998; Elley and Foster, 1996; Elley and Mangubhai, 1983) has shown that children succeed in becoming literate in English when

> . . . their classrooms are flooded with a large supply of high-interest, illustrated reading books and their teachers are shown simple methods of ensuring that the children interact regularly and productively with these books . . . . The research done on the book-based approach shows that it works well in a diverse set of countries and cultures, that it accelerates all aspects of children's language growth, that it does not require many hours of teacher training, and that it is not necessarily expensive. (Elley, 1998, 1–2)

In his projects, Elley provides a supply of appropriate books. He also organizes training for the teachers to enable them to use the books in a wide variety of ways, duplicating authentic activities such as bedtime-story reading. This helps the students learn to read and helps them learn English:

> The central approach used in all these studies is the method usually referred to as shared reading. This is a method of sharing a good book with a class, several times, in such a way that the students are read to by the teacher, as in a bedtime story. They then talk about the book, they read it together, they act out the story, they draw parts of it and write their own captions, they rewrite the story with different characters or events, and they use the text of the book to study new vocabulary, grammar, and other language features. (Elley, 1998, 2)

In the programs Elley has set up, teachers help students join the literacy club by providing many demonstrations as they read to and with their students. These students are able to acquire literacy because they have access to books, and their teachers use strategies to ensure that the books become comprehensible input. Elley's studies, in fact, provide powerful evidence for the claim that language, including written language, is acquired rather than learned.

Additional Research

Other studies confirm that reading achievement is related to book access. McQuillan (1998) reports on several studies that show that access to books leads to better reading. In one study (Ramos and Krashen, 1998), the researchers found that taking elementary school children who had little exposure to books to the library made a huge difference in their reading and interest in reading. Another study (Worthy, 1996) found that middle school students who read infrequently reported they had limited access to books of interest at home and a lack of opportunities to read for pleasure at school. These students did not dislike reading but they did lack access, time, and choice for pleasure reading.

LeMoine et al. (1997) categorized California schools as high-achieving or low-achieving, based on test scores. High-achieving schools allowed more visits to the school library. In addition, only 47 percent of the low-achieving schools allowed children to take books home, compared to 73 percent of the high-achieving urban schools and 100 percent of the high-achieving suburban schools.

Free Voluntary Reading

Krashen's (1996) research strongly supports the importance of providing students with time for what he calls "free voluntary reading." Through a careful review of studies of both second-language readers and native English readers, he has shown convincingly that when students are allowed to choose books of interest to them, and when they are given opportunities to read, they read more and their test scores improve. Krashen's research has also shown that students who begin by reading simpler texts or series texts, such as *Sweet Valley High*, later read books with more widely-acclaimed literary merit.

Even comic books can be a good starting point. Ujiie and Krashen (1996, 6) found that:

> . . . middle school boys who did more comic book reading also read more in general, read more books, and reported that they liked reading better than those who did less comic book reading.

Access and Economics

McQuillan (1998) also reports studies that show that the number of books available to students depends on their socioeconomic status.

♦ Feitelson and Goldstein (1986), for example, found large differences in the number of age-appropriate books in the homes of middle-income and low-income children. There were ten times as many books in the middle class homes.

♦ Another study (Raz and Bryant, 1990) revealed that differences in the number of books families owned and the number of times children visited the library was related to their economic status. The middle-income children had three times as many books at home, and they made about three times as many visits to the library each month.

♦ Allington (1995) found that there were fewer books per child in school libraries of schools that served more poor children. In addition, schools serving many poor children allowed fewer visits to the school libraries.

♦ Smith, Constantino, and Krashen (1996) studied differences in access to books in the home, school, and community in three areas of Los Angeles. This study revealed huge differences in print access between economically-depressed communities and high-income areas. For example, children in Beverly Hills homes had 199 age-appropriate books in their homes, compared to 2.7 books per child in Compton and 0.4 books per child in Watts. They also found differences in the number of books in classroom, school, and public libraries. Beverly Hills' classrooms averaged 392 books, compared to Compton's 47 and Watts' 54. School libraries in Beverly Hills had 60,000 volumes, while Watts had 23,000 and Compton 16,000. Beverly Hills' public library had 200,600 volumes, while the Watts library had only 110,00 volumes and Compton had 90,000. Taken together, these figures reveal a huge difference in access to books among the students in these three communities. Not surprisingly, reading test scores in Beverly Hills are much higher than those in the other two communities.

Together, all these research studies point strongly to the importance of access to books. Quite simply, we can't build strong reading programs without adequate text resources.

Choosing Books

Teachers who develop effective reading programs provide many books for their students to read, and they give students time to read. However, teachers like Mary, Mike, and Ann realize that what keeps some students from becoming proficient readers is that they have difficulty choosing appropriate books. The next question on the Checklist for Effective Reading Instruction focuses on helping students to make good choices of books to read.

Sometimes teachers need to help their students choose appropriate books. Before she was a Title I Director, Ann was teaching in her own bilingual, multiage classroom in a low-income rural community. She soon realized that she had to help children choose books during DEAR (Drop Everything and Read) time.

During whole-group rug time, Ann and her students would talk about choosing books. Children were to choose one easy book, one medium book, and one book that was a challenge. Ann talked to the students about how the easy book should be one they knew really well, probably by heart. The medium book should be one that they knew the story and some parts, but had to work to read; and the difficult book should be one that they knew was hard for them, but that they were interested in. Ann described how she would talk about choice with her students:

I would sit with them during rug time, so that we could practice choosing appropriate books and talk about our choices. I would hold up a book and ask: "Is this an easy book or a hard book?" One of the most difficult things for my students was not to make a snap judgment from only looking at the cover. I would hold up a small book and students would all say: "Easy!" Then I would open the book, and they would see lots of text and few pictures and revise their opinions. We talked about the fact that they needed to open the book before they decided. We discussed the characteristics of books, including pictures, size of print, repetition of patterns, and their familiarity with the story. As we decided on a book as a group, I would put it in a basket marked "EASY" or "MEDIUM" or "DIFFICULT." Of course, readers in my class differed, and it was important for me to walk around the room and challenge readers for whom a MEDIUM book was too easy, for example. Eventually, students did not depend upon the baskets, but went to the shelves to pick out their books.

Teachers of older students also need to help their students make good choices. Grace teaches eighth grade in a small rural school. Students enter her class with large differences in their reading proficiency. Many of them started school speaking a language other than English, but their primary language literacy was not developed. Some can read almost any book, and others can only read books normally used at lower grades.

Grace reads to her students every day. She organizes her curriculum around themes based on big questions, such as: "What happens when cultures collide?" She collects text sets related to the themes. These text sets include multiple copies of books at different levels of difficulty. To help her students choose their books, Grace does book talks. Over several days, she presents each book, reading parts aloud, showing pages and pictures, and talking about the plot and setting of each one. She makes sure that students not only get a good sense of what the book is about, but also how difficult the book is to read. This preparation helps her students make good choices of texts. Grace also counsels her students to reinforce good choices, and to get students who have made inappropriate choices to rethink their decision.

Conclusion

In this chapter, we have discussed the importance of teachers reading to provide demonstrations for students. Students are more likely to engage in reading when they are provided with many demonstrations of others reading for pleasure or information. We also discussed sensitivity. Like Leo the late bloomer, children learn to read most easily when those around them never give them a hint that they don't expect the child to learn how to read or that reading might be hard.

Students also need access to books. We described how Ann built a school library, and we listed ways that teachers could build a classroom library as Mike did. We also emphasized the importance of choice. All readers need to learn how to choose appropriate books. When students have access to books and time to read, their proficiency increases. Students acquire literacy when they receive comprehensible input from texts.

In discussing Ann's Literacy Club, we listed a number of ways the tutors interacted with the younger students to engage them with texts. The key to this program is that the tutors help keep their partners focused on making meaning. In the next chapter, we look more closely at the central tenet of the sociopsycholinguistic theory: reading is constructing meaning. We also consider what characterizes a proficient reader.

Promoting Proficient Reading

Checklist Questions This Chapter Addresses

Question 6. Do students regard reading as meaning making at all times? That is, do they construct meaning as they read?
Question 7. Are students effective readers? That is, do they make a balanced use of all three cueing systems?
Question 8. Are students efficient readers? That is, do they make minimal use of cues to construct meaning?

The first five questions on the Checklist for Effective Reading Instruction all focus on getting students to read so they will come to value reading and value themselves as readers. The sixth question gets at the heart of effective reading instruction: finding ways to help students see that the goal is to make sense of what they are reading.

We begin this chapter by describing a unit that Cheri, the resource teacher introduced in the Introduction, has developed to help her students with their varied needs, to focus on making meaning as they read. For most of us, it seems only natural that the purpose of reading is to create meaning, whether we are reading a grocery list, our electric bill, a novel, or a college textbook. For beginning or struggling readers and for English-language learners, though, there is the danger that they will get confused about why they are reading. Teachers need to help students understand the goal of reading, as well as the procedures for building meaning from text.

Cheri's Unit: Somewhere over the Rainbow

As a resource teacher, Cheri knows she has a special responsibility to begin with her students' strengths, and she works hard to draw on the interests of her students. She does this well with her multilingual, multicultural students. She is careful to learn to pronounce their names correctly and makes a point of learning how to say key salutations in their native languages. She draws on their cultural experiences, too. For example, when she had one student of Hispanic origin, she brought into class a PBS program on Latino filmmakers. Showing this film allowed that student to share with the rest of the class connections he made with parts of the video. Her Khmer students have shared cultural traditions from Cambodia such as New Year's celebrations and native dances.

Because students are in and out of her room all day long, and Cheri is responsible for at least half of their core subject matter, she organizes her curriculum around themes. Themes provide continuity and help her students make sense of daily lessons. Cheri knows she has to help her students value reading and see reading as a meaning-making process. Few of her students view themselves as successful learners. Often, this is due to their lack of success in reading. Few of them see reading as a pleasurable activity. For that reason, she develops themes that capture their interest.

Cheri launched one theme by writing an intriguing title, "Somewhere Over the Rainbow," on the board and having students predict what they would be studying. At first they guessed things like, "Wizard of Oz" and "Pot of Gold," but eventually they came up with the idea of color. Then, Cheri put up a large piece of butcher paper and asked students to tell her what they already knew about color. Students responded with:

"We use our eyes and light to see color."
"We can't feel it or taste it or smell it."
"We can mix colors to make other colors."

After this last comment, Cheri prompted students to get more specific by saying, "I bet you know what happens if blue and yellow paint get mixed!" Soon, students had come up with lots they knew and also several "wonders": "I've always wondered why . . ."

Next, the class began to list all the color names they could think of. They used resources in the room such as boxes of crayons, colored pencils, clothing catalogs, and paint card samples and completed a list of nearly one hundred color names that ranged from basic colors, like yellow, to unusual colors such as azurite, cerulean, and vermilion. As they completed the list, students started to talk about where color names came from. They discovered different sources, such as plant names like fuchsia and violet, and names of metals such as gold and silver. As they looked through catalogues, they noticed that some color names are associated with fruit so Cheri helped them create a list that included banana yellow, cherry red, and plum. The students decided that the public probably would not buy products advertised with vegetable names such as potato brown or broccoli green. All this attention to vocabulary was especially helpful for Cheri's second language students.

As the unit progressed, Cheri read different texts to the students that supported key concepts. A book that Cheri's students especially liked was *Color* by Alison Cole (1993). This book, published in association with the National Gallery of Art in Washington, includes fascinating information about color from art around the world. Another interesting book was *How is a Crayon Made?* (Charles, 1988) and the Spanish version, *¿Cómo se hace un crayón?* (Oz, 1993), which shows through text and photographs the process for making crayons. Two other books that include both science concepts and different projects with colors are *Science for Fun: Light and Color* (Gibson, 1994) and *Light and Color* (Walker, 1993). One particularly fascinating book for students is *Color, Color, Color, Color* (Heller, 1995). This book not only discusses key concepts in delightful rhyme, but demonstrates the concepts using colored plastic overlays and beautiful illustrations with brilliant colors. Among other things, the book explains how printers use four ink stages, using first yellow, then magenta, then cyan blue, and finally black to create all the printed colors we see. Heller also explains how printers apply primary colors in dots, combining them to create secondary colors:

> The printers are some kind of wizard I think.
> In minuscule dots they apply all the ink.
> They apply all the ink to a surface that's white.
> HOKUS and POKUS—Behold! What a sight . . .
> So yellows . . . magentas . . . and cyan blues . . . are the primary hues that
>   printers use,
> and the combination of any two produces a secondary hue.
> The secondary colors seen
> are—PRESTO and CHANGE-O—
> orange, purple, and green. (Heller, 1995, 15, 16, 18 and 19).

Cheri's students looked at the Sunday comics, labels at the bottom of cereal and cracker boxes, and other printed products to find the marks of the three primary hues that printers use in the printing process. They were amazed that these markers are found on almost all color-printed texts.

Cheri's students do a variety of interesting experiments and activities that encourage concept development during their unit on "Somewhere Over the Rainbow." Some are described below:

♦ Mix food coloring in clear plastic cups and make generalizations about primary, secondary, and intermediate colors in follow-up discussions.

♦ Create a paper weaving with strips of colored paper on either white or black backgrounds. Hang the weavings and discuss the different effects and moods that are produced.

♦ Use color wheels so students can explore the concepts of triads, complementary colors, tint, shade, tone, and pastel.

♦ Have students use prisms to shine rainbows on a white wall or white paper and overlay one rainbow with another. Discuss the results, which include the ideas of subtractive color and additive color. Talk about how a color TV works.

♦ Make spinners three inches in diameter on white cardboard and hang them on a string. Have students color the markers and see the different blending effects they can create using dots, lines, or zigzags.

♦ Construct a "color guess box" by cutting two holes in the sides of a cardboard box. Use duct tape to attach the cut-off sleeves of a shirt to the holes. This keeps students from seeing through the holes. Inside the box, place items such as a carrot, peanuts in their shells, a crayon, and a leaf. The students cannot see the items, but they can touch them through the sleeves of the shirt. As they try to guess the colors of the different objects, they talk about which items they can make reasonable guesses for and which objects are impossible to guess.

♦ Have students take some standard color-blindness tests found in many library books. Talk about seeing the hidden patterns in the test. Talk about how different the world is for those who are color-blind and how it affects their lives. Talk about how animals have different color perceptions.

Because she wants to be sure to promote language development, Cheri is careful to include activities that focus on language. Below are listed some of the language-related activities Cheri and her students carry out during the color unit:

♦ Colors symbolism—Students brainstorm different colors that carry a symbolic meaning, such as black being used for mourning, white for brides, red signaling stop or danger, yellow indicating warning, and red, white and blue representing U.S. nationalism. Cheri points out that sometimes colors have different meanings in different cultures or languages. In some Spanish-speaking cultures, for example, an off-color joke is referred to as a "a green joke," and in Chinese, yellow represents health.

♦ Color expressions—Students discuss common color expressions, including both the literal and figurative meanings. Some examples include "looking white as a ghost," "having blue blood," "being green with envy," and "being given a golden opportunity."

♦ Color related to feelings and emotions—Students discuss how some colors are related to how we feel, such as blue indicating sad, cold, or depressed or red suggesting anger, or being hot or embarrassed.

♦ Color and holidays—Students discuss how some colors are associated with holidays, such as green with St. Patrick's Day, green and red with Christmas, and orange and black with Halloween.

Through all the activities, Cheri's students read, write, and talk. Many of the activities result in lists that are hung around the room and used for discussion and further reference. Cheri's students are constantly engaged in activities that have meaning and purpose for them. In fact, they often get so excited about what they are doing in class, they take the activities to show their friends and family. Despite the many challenges her students face as learners, Cheri is helping them become empowered learners and leading them towards the literacy they need.

Cheri helps her students realize that the goal of reading is to make meaning. Krashen (1999) has reviewed a number of studies that compare students in classes with a focus on meaning with similar students in classes with a focus on building the skills needed to recognize words. These studies show that students in meaning-centered classes do more real reading, have better attitudes toward reading, and read more.

For example, Morrow, O'Connor, and Smith (1990) report on two groups of "at risk" kindergarten children who received an extra hour of instruction each day. The instruction for one group centered on learning the alphabet, although there was also some storybook reading. The instruction for the other group focused on meaningful reading. Teachers read to children and involved them in activities with literature. At the end of a year, the meaning-based group did much better than the other group on tests of reading comprehension and story-retelling. If the goal of reading is to construct meaning from texts, this group met that goal much better than the group that focused on skills.

By describing the effective practices of teachers like Cheri, Debbie, Mary, Ann, Francisco, Erin, Janet, and Veronica, we have shown some of the components of reading programs that help students focus on meaning. However some students who try to focus on meaning are not successful readers. In the next section, we consider the factors involved in proficient reading.

Reading Proficiency

Questions 7 and 8 on the Checklist for Effective Reading Instruction focus on proficiency. Figure 5–1 summarizes the essential features of proficiency. Below, we discuss each of the key elements.

Reading Proficiency	
Defined as	Effectiveness + efficiency
Achieved by	Balanced, minimal use of 3 cueing systems
Attitude toward error	Errors differ in quality
Response to error	Help readers keep focus on comprehension

Figure 5–1 Reading Proficiency

Definition of Proficiency

Proficient readers are both effective and efficient. Effective readers make a balanced use of all three cue systems. They are like well-tuned engines that fire on all cylinders, not just one or two. Ineffective readers often focus too much on one cueing system and miss the cues that come from the other two. Often, they pay too much attention to graphophonics. Their miscues result in sentences that don't sound like English and don't make sense.

Proficient readers are also efficient. Efficient readers use only as much information as necessary to construct meaning. The idea of a minimal use of cues strikes some teachers as wrong somehow. Shouldn't readers use every cue? Our contention is that good readers use only what is necessary. Processing more cues would only slow them down. To continue our analogy with a car engine, effective readers fire on all the cylinders, not just some of the cylinders, and efficient readers use just enough fuel to power the engine. They don't waste fuel. Another analogy would be that of good nutrition. When we eat well, we eat a balanced diet. We do not leave out a major food group, but we also take in just enough calories and nutrients to remain healthy and function at a high level. We can't stay healthy if we eat all the calories that are available.

Inefficient readers pay too much attention to details and correct even when their errors (or miscues) do not interrupt meaning. For example, in her reading Ann makes the following miscue:

> ©bounce
> . . . and bound up the apartment house stairs

Even though there is little difference between *bounce* and *bound* up the stairs, Ann goes back and corrects her miscue. This slows down her reading. Since she is less efficient, she is also less proficient. As students like Ann move through the grades, the amount and complexity of reading they are expected to complete increases, and if they read too slowly and carefully, trying to get every word right, they fall behind in their academic work.

Often, English language learners focus too much on details, as Ann does here. Students who are still learning English don't have full control of any of the three cueing systems, and they may lack background knowledge for certain topics or types of stories. As a result, they often slow down and work hard to understand the details. Frequently, they miss the big picture. They are so busy getting the sounds and words right that they miss the syntactic and semantic cues that would help them build meaning for the whole text. Teachers can help such students by previewing the reading with them and then asking general comprehension questions, such as, "What do you remember?" after they read.

Errors and Proficiency

All readers make errors. However, all errors are not equally bad. They differ in quality. If the goal of reading is to construct meaning, then errors that result in a loss of meaning are problematic, but errors that retain meaning are not. When Ann substituted *bounce* for *bound*, her miscue did not cause a loss of meaning. On the other hand, if she had substituted a word like *board*, then the miscue would have resulted in a sentence that does not follow an English syntactic pattern and does not make sense. The way to respond to error, then, depends on the kind of error. The goal is to keep readers focused on making sense.

Teachers can assess reading by using a procedure like miscue analysis. Teachers then plan strategy lessons to help students build greater proficiency. We examine miscue analysis and strategy lessons in the following chapter. (See Chapter Eight for a discussion of the problems associated with the practice of having students do round-robin oral reading, with the teacher or other students correcting errors.)

It is especially important for teachers to keep English-language learners focused on meaning. Often, when students are reading in their second language, they attend primarily to the surface features of the text. In classes that stress oral reading, these students concentrate on accurate pronunciation. Teachers sometimes try to help these English-language learners by working with them on their pronunciation, an area where their English is noticeably nonstandard. The problem with this focus is that language minority students often come to believe that reading proficiency depends on pronouncing each word correctly, not on meaning.

Teachers who follow the Checklist for Effective Reading Instruction know that reading proficiency develops when students stay focused on meaning. In the next section, we describe a unit that Sandra taught to help her students become more proficient readers.

Sandra's Classroom

All my students are Hispanic. They are migrant kids who mainly have not been in school in Mexico, or they had maybe a few years of school before they came to the United States. The main concern to help these kids is that they stay out of school for a long time. Even when they are living here, they leave me in May to follow crops in the north and return in September. Many also miss in December and January, when their families go back to Mexico.

Sandra's "Newcomers" class is for students from nine to twelve years old who stay with her all day for all their subjects. These students are designated as fourth, fifth, and sixth graders based on their ages, but their interrupted schooling has left many with little or no literacy in their first language which is either Spanish or Mixteco, an indigenous language of Southern Mexico. Her Mixteco students usually understand Spanish, although they lack literacy in any language. All the students must learn to negotiate school in English.

Sandra is the Spanish/English bilingual teacher we described in the Introduction, so she can provide students with previews and review in Spanish of English lessons. Because her students are newcomers with little previous schooling, Sandra organizes her day with a consistent routine and organizes her curriculum around themes. Routines and thematic teaching help her students predict what to expect and allows them to concentrate on learning to read, write, and problem-solve. Figure 5–2 shows Sandra's daily schedule.

Sandra's students do much of their work in groups that she organizes heterogeneously, so that students with different abilities can help one another. For example, her Mixteco students, who have had little schooling, shine when illustrating publications and are supported in language activities by others in their groups. When students work in centers, Sandra is also sure to pair them so that a strong student can help a student who needs more support.

Whenever possible, Sandra encourages students to take responsibility for leading activities. This makes her class more learner-centered. Students lead the review of the calendar, which includes writing pertinent information on the whiteboard. Since her students are all English learners who need literacy support, Sandra has them sing songs daily, reading the words

Daily Schedule Mrs. Mercuri's Class (4–6 Newcomers)	
8:10–8:30	News of the Day Attendance Calendar Date Song of the Week
8:30–9:00	Writers Notebook
9:00–9:10	Writes Notebook Sharing Time
9:10–9:45	Read Aloud/Shared Reading Phonemic Awareness (P.E. twice a week)
9:45–10:15	Recess
10:15–11:50	Centers(*) *Math* *Listening Center* Silent Reading/Library *Computer (Editing or Phonics)* *ELD/Spelling/Phonics* *Art* *Guided Reading (Mini-lessons/Critical Thinking and Comprehension Strategies according to students' needs)*
1:50–12:50	Lunch
12:50–1:30	Last Rotation in Centers
1:30–1:50	D.E.A.R. Time/Readers Theater
1:50–2:30	Math
2:30–3:00	Science
3:00–3:05	Dismissal

(*) Students spend 20 minutes at each center.
Students participate in other activities like Computer lab on Fridays and P.E. twice a week.

Figure 5–2 Sandra's Daily Schedule

as one student tracks on a large poster.

Sandra provides ample time daily for students to read and write. She reads to and with students several times during the day. Sandra has collected multiple copies of books, so that during shared reading, she and her students can read limited-text books, poetry, and chapter books together.

During guided reading, Sandra works with different groups, supporting early readers with high-interest limited-text books that are predictable and have patterns. Sandra engages her more proficient readers in literature studies with chapter books. As they discuss these books, Sandra demonstrates comprehension strategies and encourages students to analyze and think critically.

At times, Sandra helps her students focus on the graphophonic system. One of the centers that students can choose from is a CD-ROM program that has many activities that focus on letter patterns, sounds, and spellings. In addition, Sandra uses examples of miscues from her students' reading during class discussions. She puts an interesting miscue on the overhead, and she and the class discuss it. If the miscue was a substitution, the class might discuss if the substituted word begins and ends the same as the word in the text. Sandra knows that phonics programs in English are difficult for her students because their pronunciation of English is not yet conventional, and she worries that too much focus on phonics will cause her students to lose the emphasis on reading for meaning. Nevertheless, she also knows that it is important for her students to learn to use all three cueing systems to become proficient readers, as they construct meaning from texts. (See Chapter Eight for a discussion of the difference between helping students develop their control of the graphophonic cue system and the direct teaching of phonemic awareness and phonics.)

Sandra's Immigrant Unit

Sandra provides stability for her students with a regular daily routine and by organizing around themes. Sandra begins her year with a unit on immigrants. She explains why she does this.

> Most of these kids have come to the United States. We know what they are going through. Being an immigrant myself, I know how they feel. Talking about those issues is going to make them feel comfortable in the classroom . . . to feel they are not alone. A lot of people through the years have been immigrants in this country . . . in different situations. This country was made by immigrants.

The topic is relevant to her students, and the readings and activities promote literacy for all the students. Sandra organizes her units around literature. She chooses books that offer many connections with students' lives. Several of the books are also available in Spanish or are bilingual versions. This allows Sandra to use the Spanish version as a preview of the content to be discussed in Spanish or English. Sandra and her students do webbing and Venn diagrams as they look at key concepts in the readings, comparing and contrasting stories and relating them to their own experiences. For example, *How Many Days to America* (Bunting, 1988) was a catalyst for students to tell their own stories about how they came to this country. Students told these often-traumatic stories and then wrote them. Through sharing and writing, students came to appreciate their own strengths and those of their classmates.

Figure 5–3 is a bibliography with brief annotations of the books Sandra and her students read during their immigrant unit.

Ada, A. F. 1993. *My Name is María Isabel*. New York: Atheneum Books. The wonderful story of a girl whose pride in her own name causes her problems at school.

————. 1997. *Gathering the Sun*. New York: Lothrop, Lee & Shepard. This Spanish/English bilingual alphabet is filled with beautiful poetry and art work reflective of Mexican culture, and especially the experiences of migrant families.

Ada, A. F., Harris, V. J., and Hopkins, L. B. 1993. *A Chorus of Cultures: Developing Literacy Through Multicultural Poetry*. Carmel, Calif.: Hampton-Brown Books. This rich resource books is full of poetry, songs, games, and other activities to celebrate diverse cultures and includes immigrant poems written by children.

Anzaldúa, G. 1993. *Friends from the Other Side*. San Francisco: Children's Book Press. This bilingual Spanish/English story tells of children living in border towns between Mexico and the United States.

Carden, M. and M. Cappellini. 1997. *Soy de dos lugares: Poesía juvenil*. (English version: *I Am of Two Places: Children's Poetry*) Crystal Lake, Ill.: Rigby. The poetry in this book is written from the heart by children of Latin American origin living in the United States.

Cohen, B. 1983. *Molly's Pilgrim*. New York: Lothrop, Lee & Shepard Books. This classic Thanksgiving story tells of a Russian immigrant girl in the United States who learns that she is a real pilgrim.

Dooley, N. 1993. *Todo el mundo cocina arroz*. (English version: *Everyone Cooks Rice* 1991) New York: Scholastic. A sister searches for her brother through the kitchens of her multicultural neighborhood, trying the rice dishes from each culture.

Freedman, R. 1980. *Immigrant Kids*. New York: Scholastic. This pictorial history of immigrant children in the late 1800s and early 1900s gives readers an idea of how young immigrants in the United States lived.

Friedman, I. 1984. *How My Parents Learned to Eat*. Boston: Houghton Mifflin. The author explains how her mother, originally from Japan, and her father, from the

United States, learned to eat using utensils from each culture, learning to appreciate each others' culture in the process.

Garza, C. L. 1990. *Family Pictures: Cuadros de familia.* San Francisco: Children's Book Press. The Hispanic author/artist illustrates and describes memorable family and community events from her childhood growing up in Texas. (Bilingual Spanish/English book)

————. 1996. *In My Family: En mi familia.* San Francisco: Children's Book Press. The Hispanic author/artist offers a second book of memorable family and community events from her childhood growing up in Texas. (Bilingual Spanish/English book)

Herminio Acuña, M. 1997. *Vestiimos con orgullo.* (English version: *Dressing with Pride*) Crystal Lake, Ill.: Rigby. Traditional dress of families from Vietnamese, Hmong, Chinese, Japanese, and Khmer cultures are depicted in photos and described in this book.

Keane, S. M. 1997 *Querida abuelita* (English version: *Dear Abuelita*), Crystal Lake, Ill.: Rigby. A new immigrant boy writes to his grandmother of his experiences in his new home in a city in California.

Knight, M. 1993. *Who Belongs Here? An American Story.* Gardiner, Maine: Tilbury House. In this book, readers find the story of a Khmer boy's struggles for acceptance in a U.S. school, woven with historical facts about this multicultural/multilingual nation.

Levinson, R. 1987. *Mira, cómo salen las estrellas.* Madrid, Spain: Ediciones Altea. (English version: *Watch the Stars Come Out.* 1985. New York: E.P. Dutton.) A brother and sister travel by ship to America, where they join their family as immigrants.

Maitland, K. 1997. *Una sorpresa para Mónica.* (English version: *A Surprise for Monica*) Crystal Lake, Ill.: Rigby. A librarian befriends a migrant child and encourages her to tell her stories.

Nguyen, A. O. and P. Abello 1997. *Nuestro viaje hacia la libertad.* (English version: *Our Trip to Freedom*) Crystal Lake, Ill.: Rigby. A grandfather tells of how his family escaped from Vietnam during the war to come to America for freedom.

Polaco, P. 1988. *The Keeping Quilt.* New York: Simon and Schuster Books for Young Readers. A quilt made from material brought over from Russia is handed down by a Jewish family to remember their homeland and immigrant lives.

Puncel, M. 1997. *El amigo nuevo.* Boston: Houghton Mifflin. A young boy from Japan moves into a neighborhood and makes friends with the English-speaking children, sharing his culture and language.

Say, A. 1997. *La jornada de abuelo.* (English version: *Grandfather's Journey*) Boston: Houghton Mifflin. The author shares how his grandfather came to America, settled here, and returned to Japan. The grandfather's story gives the author roots.

Figure 5–3 Immigrant Unit Bibliography

Sandra engages her students in many different projects during her units. Below are some of the activities she uses during the immigrant study.

♦ ABC of ALL—Students brainstorm words they know in English that relate to the theme. For example, "I is for immigrants. We are all immigrants." This list grows throughout the unit. This becomes an alphabet book.

♦ Family Tree—Students interview their families and make a family tree to share with the class.

♦ Map of Immigrants—With each immigrant literature piece, students locate on the map where the immigrants in the story come from.

♦ Research of Native Country—Students ask their families about towns and states where they come from. They look these places up on a large map and in reference books, researching population, industries, crops, and geographic features. They make connections with their own memories of where they came from. Then, they graph some of the information and present their findings to the class.

♦ Travel Brochures—The teacher brings in a variety of travel brochures. Using the information they have gathered from the research on their native towns and states, the students design a travel brochure of their region. They type the copy and add art work, using classroom computers.

♦ International Recipe Book—Students interview family members about traditional recipes. After a discussion of measurements of ingredients, students work with family members to write a recipe. The students put together a class recipe book complete with a narrative about where each recipe comes from. The activity is celebrated with a pot luck. Students invite family members and bring food created using the recipes from the recipe book.

♦ Multicultural Corner—Students and family members bring in artifacts, photos, cloth, or other items to display and talk about in class and to decorate the room during Open House.

Sandra bases her curriculum around the Checklist for Effective Reading Instruction. Her students know that the goal of reading is to construct meaning from texts. Sandra's reading program is designed to help her students become proficient readers. Sandra also knows the importance of assessing her students' reading abilities. In the next chapter, we explain how teachers can use miscue analysis to assess reading proficiency and plan strategy instruction.

Assessing Reading

Checklist Question This Chapter Addresses

Question 9: Are students provided with appropriate strategy lessons if they experience difficulties in their reading?

Some students develop high levels of reading proficiency with little assistance from teachers or other adults. Other students, though, struggle with reading. Teachers who follow the Checklist for Effective Reading Instruction recognize the importance of assessing students' reading and planning appropriate instruction. In this chapter, we first introduce miscue analysis as an authentic assessment tool. Then we show how teachers can use the results of miscue analysis to provide strategy lessons to assist struggling readers.

Using Miscue Analysis to Assess Reading Proficiency

Miscue analysis is a procedure teachers and reading specialists use to assess a student's proficiency. This assessment can be used to determine how well a reader is using the three cueing systems. Miscue analysis is not intended to be used with all students, only those who are having difficulties with their reading. If a teacher can use informal observation to determine why the student is struggling, there is no need for formal assessment. Miscue analysis might be used with only two or three students in any one class. Teachers can use the results to determine what instructional help these readers need and decide on an appropriate strategy. Miscue analysis also gives teachers important insights into the reading process itself. Wilde (2000) has written a book that explains miscue analysis very clearly: *Miscue Analysis Made Easy*.

During a miscue session, the teacher sits with the student. They each have a copy of a short story or content text that the student has not seen before. Miscue analysis is always carried out using a complete text that is slightly hard for the student to read. It is only by giving students slightly difficult texts that teachers can figure out where they are having trouble. The student reads the text aloud and then retells what is remembered. Usually, teachers tape record the session and also take notes as the student reads and retells.

After the session, the teacher analyzes the miscues the reader made. Miscues are unexpected responses to a text. When a reader omits a word, inserts a word, substitutes one word for another, or reverses words, that is a miscue because it is not what we expect. Teachers also note whether or not students reread and attempt to correct miscues. Y. Goodman and colleagues (Goodman, et al., 1987, 1996) have developed different procedures for analyzing miscues and the retelling and using this information to plan appropriate instruction.

One procedure that is often used by classroom teachers involves first marking down each miscue and then going back through the text to determine what the miscues show about the reader's use of the three cueing systems. The teacher reads each sentence as the student finally produced it. If the student made a miscue, the sentence is read with the miscue; but if the reader corrected it, the sentence is read as correct. Then the teacher asks the following questions (Goodman, et al., 1987, 107–108):

♦ Is the sentence syntactically (grammatically) acceptable in the reader's dialect and within the context of the entire selection?
  If the answer is "yes," the teacher asks:

♦ Is the sentence semantically acceptable in the reader's dialect and within the context of the entire selection?
  Again, if the answer is "yes," the teacher asks:

♦ Does the sentence, as finally produced by the reader, change the meaning of the selection?

These first three questions help teachers determine how well the student is using syntactic and semantic cues and how well the student is constructing a conventional meaning for the text. By "conventional meaning," we refer to a meaning that most readers would agree with. These questions are asked of each sentence. If there are no miscues or if they are corrected, the sentence would be marked "yes," "yes," and "no." When miscues occur, teachers analyze the resulting sentences. For example, Juan made the following miscues during one section of his reading:

plan   don't

(#1) You broke my plane! (#2) "I didn't mean to," Billy said.

Ⓒ

Vicky pick   broke plan

(#3) Victor picked up his broken plane.

Juan makes several substitutions here and only corrects one of them. How would we evaluate these sentences?

#1 YN—Juan's substitution of *plan* for *plane* results in a sentence that sounds like English, because he substituted a noun for a noun. However, it doesn't make any sense, so it is marked "No" for semantics. We don't ask about meaning change unless we answer "Yes" for the first two questions, so we leave that blank.

#2 NN—Substituting *don't* for *didn't* works if we only look at this sentence. However, miscues are evaluated in the context of the whole story, and this shift to present tense doesn't fit here because all the dialogue is in the past. For that reason, we give it a "No" on syntax, and then we automatically give it a "No" on semantics, since we don't go on to ask the second question unless we answer the first one with "Yes."

#3 NN—Even though Juan corrects *broke*, the other miscues result in a sentence that is not acceptable syntactically or semantically.

If these sentences are typical of Juan's reading, we can conclude that he is not a proficient reader. After teachers evaluate all the sentences, they compile the results and find the percentage of sentences that are syntactically acceptable, the percentage that are semantically acceptable, and the percentage that change meaning. These results, along with a holistic retelling score, help teachers see how well readers are using the syntactic and semantic cueing systems.

Miscue analysis also provides information about graphophonics. In addition to the three questions listed above, teachers look at each case in which a reader substitutes a word or a nonsense word and asks:

♦ How much does the miscue look like the text item?

This question is normally answered by dividing the word into three parts. Most one-syllable words can be divided by using the beginning consonant or consonant cluster, the middle vowel, and the ending. Thus, *plane* would be split up as *pl-a-ne*. Longer words can often be divided fairly easily as well. For example, *broken* would be *br-o-ken*. for short words like *to* the graphic similarity is high if one part is the same. If one part is the same, there is some similarity. If two parts are the same, there is a high degree of similarity. If the miscue and the text word are completely different, there in no similarity. All of Juan's miscues show a high degree of graphic similarity. The substitutions include many of the same letters as the words in the text. More complex procedures enable teachers to consider both graphics and sound similarity, using a similar method to determine sound similarity.

As a result of a complete miscue analysis (one that includes all the sentences, not just these three), we might rate Juan as low in syntax and semantics and high in graphophonics. This suggests that he needs strategy lessons that help him check to see if the sentences he produces sound like English and make sense. He doesn't need more work on phonics, because he is overusing the graphophonic system already. We provide examples of strategy lessons at the end of this chapter. (See Chapter Eight for a discussion of the differences between graphophonics and phonics).

Miscue analysis is appropriate to use with English language learners. The procedure can be done to assess reading in their native language or in English if they have begun reading books in English. It must be noted, however, that if the miscue analysis is carried out in English, miscues are assessed on the basis of the reader's dialect—the usual way the student speaks English. For example, teachers of students who speak one of the Southeast Asian languages, such as Hmong or Lao, will not be surprised if students read "He walks" as "He walk." These students have not made a reading miscue. They have simply translated the English text into their normal oral language pattern. Since this is how the student would say the sentence in conversation, it is not rated as a miscue.

Miscue analysis helps teachers understand reading, and it is also a valuable tool for teachers who wish to gain more insight into the processes a struggling reader is using. It can help the teacher evaluate the reader's use of each of the three systems and plan appropriate instruction. If several teachers at a school site or in a district carry out miscue analyses on their students and then compare the results, they can use this information to evaluate the school or district reading curriculum and decide on possible changes in instructional approach.

Using the Results of Miscue Analysis

David asked teachers in his class on reading assessment to choose a struggling reader from their class and conduct a miscue analysis. Each teacher chose one student, had them read a complete story, and analyzed the miscues.

The chart, Figure 6-1, shows the results of their analyses of twenty-two students. The second column shows the percent of miscues that were

Student Number	Graphics	Syntax	Semantics
1	100	35	27
2	100	48	26
3	100	52	46
4	100	60	34
5	98	42	30
6	97	34	27
7	97	46	52
8	95	31	32
9	93	53	46
10	92	19	24
11	92	38	41
12	92	60	56
13	91	64	76
14	90	62	73
15	89	51	20
16	87	54	66
17	87	61	65
18	85	58	26
19	85	61	45
20	84	51	56
21	83	56	68
22	82	58	46

Figure 6–1 Miscue Analysis Results

marked "Yes" for graphics because they had high graphic similarity (two parts of three were the same, as in *plan* and *plane*) or some graphic similarity (one part was the same, as in *plot* and *plane*). Notice how high these troubled readers scored. The average score was 92 percent. Even for the lowest student in this category, 82 percent of the miscues were words that looked like the words in the text. The high scores for graphic similarity suggest that these troubled readers may have had a great deal of previous instruction that focused on phonics.

The third column lists the scores for syntax. Students are given a "Yes" on syntax if they put a word that is the right part of speech (like *plan* for *plane*) and fits the whole sentence, or if they put in a word that could fit in the sentence up to that point. For example, in the following sentence, the substitution of *book* fits with the first part of the sentence even though it doesn't fit the whole sentence when *plane* follows.

book
Victor picked up his broken plane.

The scores for syntax were much lower than those for graphic similarity. The average was only 50 percent. That means that these students only put in words that resulted in sentences that followed English word order patterns half the time. This is a very low score. The sentences that these students read didn't sound like English. In fact, the students with the highest scores in graphics, scored below the group average on syntax.

Similarly, the semantics scores for these struggling readers were very low. Readers get a "Yes" for semantics if the miscue results in a sentence that makes sense (such as Ann's *bounce* for *bound*) or if the part up to the miscue makes sense, as in the following sentence:

placed
Victor picked up his broken plane.

The first part of the sentence, *Victor placed* makes sense, but the whole sentence doesn't. Even giving credit for these miscues that work with part of the sentence, we see that the semantics scores were very low. The average here was only 45 percent. That means that these readers lost meaning on 55 percent of their miscues. Not surprisingly, the students had a hard time retelling the stories. The results suggest that these students need strategy lessons that help them focus on making meaning as they read.

Proficient readers make a balanced use of all three cueing systems. Although researchers using miscue analysis would not attempt to set absolute score levels for proficiency, teachers could reasonably expect proficient readers to score at least at the 80 percent level for each of the three systems. It seems clear that none of the readers whose scores are listed above meet this criteria for proficiency. If these scores had all come from one school or one district, teachers and reading specialists could use the results to plan changes in the reading instructional plan.

Miscue analysis is a powerful tool for gaining insights into the reading process and for evaluating individual readers. However, as Y. Goodman and her colleagues (1987, 147–148) comment:

> No single measure, including one RMI [reading miscue inventory] can be used exclusively to evaluate readers. The text the reader is asked to read constitutes a major influence. If the text is not well written or has not been selected with the interest, age, and background of the reader taken into consideration, scores are likely to be depressed. Proficiency is influenced not only by how well readers control the process, but also by how interested they are in the material, their purpose for reading, and the background information they bring to the reading. One student may be a highly proficient reader of novels, but only moderately proficient in the reading of knitting instructions. Another student may construct a great deal of meaning while reading historical fiction, but respond to a history textbook with nonproficient strategies.

From a sociopsycholinguistic view, reading proficiency depends on both the reader and the text. In assessing proficiency, it is important to remember that the choice of a text influences the results. Students need experiences with a variety of texts representing different genres to increase their overall proficiency.

The benefit of using miscue analysis to evaluate reading is that teachers can use the results to decide what kinds of strategy lessons might best help struggling readers. Generally, lessons are chosen that build on readers' strengths and also help them make better use of background knowledge or cueing systems that they are not utilizing fully. In the next section, we look more closely at strategy lessons.

Reading Strategy Instruction

In their book, *Reading Strategies: Focus on Comprehension,* Y. Goodman and her colleagues (1996, 47) list several key features of reading strategy instruction:

♦ It is public and takes place in a social setting.

♦ It highlights one of the language cueing systems within a text that integrates language authentically.

♦ It focuses on one of the natural strategies within the reading process.

♦ It supports and focuses the responsibilities of the reader.

Strategy lessons are social. They usually involve small groups of students who can learn from the teacher and from one another. Each lesson highlights one cueing system and uses a text that provides students with opportunities to focus on that cueing system. Lessons are designed to support readers and help them develop the strategies they should use. The lessons help readers assume the responsibility for using the strategies to construct meaning as they read. According to Goodman and her colleagues (50):

> The reading strategy lesson is constructed to help readers gain information from a language cueing system that they may not be using adequately or that they may believe they should not use. The instruction makes readers aware of the reading process. The structure of the lesson moves readers back into low gear where they can focus on the process as well as on the meaning.

Teachers want to keep readers focused on meaning, because students acquire literacy as they receive written messages that are comprehensible. However, there are times when it helps readers to bring their strategies to a conscious level. In this process, they may refine the strategies they have, or they may realize they need to add new strategies. For example, a student like Juan might become aware that while he is using visual knowledge quite well, he is not using syntactic or semantic cues. If his teacher involves him in a lesson that focuses on the syntactic or semantic systems Juan can use the new strategy to strengthen his use of the other two cue systems. *Reading Strategies* contains strategy lessons to help students use background knowledge as well as each of the cue systems. This book is a rich source of ideas and examples that any teacher could find useful. Many of the lessons include short texts created to highlight one of the cue systems. The lessons also include ideas for extensions and expansions, so that they can be used with students of different ages and different proficiency levels.

Another source of reading strategy lessons is D. Goodman's (1999) book, *The Reading Detective Club*. This book provides a good explanation of how to create strategy lessons based on miscue analysis. It includes many different lessons teachers can use directly with students. The lessons are imaginative and engaging, making Goodman's book an important resource for teachers.

Strategy lessons usually highlight one of the cueing systems. Below we describe sample lessons, developed by knowledgeable classroom teachers, that focus on graphophonics, syntax, and semantics.

Strategy Lessons: Using Graphophonic Cues

Lesson One

Debbie, whose daily schedule we highlighted in Chapter Two, begins her year validating students. Through activities utilizing their names, she brings graphophonics to the conscious level. Since Debbie has first through third graders, she wants to help beginning and struggling readers and at the same time encourage students to get to know one another. She uses students' names as a focus of linguistic study and reinforces the importance of peoples' names through the reading of quality literature.

Students sign in each day as they enter the classroom. Olders help youngers think about their names, including beginning letters and ending letters. Students also find their own name tags, comparing their names to others' in the class.

During rug time, Debbie and her students consider their classmates' names. They chart the length of first and last names and discuss common and uncommon lengths of those words. They look at beginning and ending letters in names. They note the frequency of vowels and consonants and discuss what letters can be expected in what locations in words, including things like ending or beginning words with vowels.

Debbie highlights the significance of names by reading books in which names play an important role, such as *My Name is María Isabel* (Ada, 1993), *Wilfrid Gordon McDonald Partridge* (Fox, 1985), and *Amelia's Road*

(Altman, 1993). Figure 6–2 lists the books in Debbie's names text set.

Ada, A. 1993. *My Name is María Isabel*. New York: Atheneum Books.

Altman, L. 1993. *Amelia's Road*. New York: Lee & Low Books Inc.

Blos, J. 1987. *Old Henry*. New York: William Morrow.

Bradman, T. 1998. *Michael*. Pomfret, Vt.: Trafalgar Square.

Chesworth, M. 1996. *Archibald Frisby*. New York: Farrar, Strauss and Giroux Inc.

Fox, M. 1985. *Wilfrid Gordon McDonald Partridge*. Brooklyn, N.Y.: Kane-Miller.

Henkes, K. 1991. *Chrysanthemum*. New York: William Morrow.

Patterson, K. 1994. *Flip-Flop Girl*. Dutton: New York.

Figure 6–2 Names Text Set

Lesson Two

In another lesson, students look at a passage that contains several words with different spellings of the *k* sound. They work in small groups to make lists of these words. The teacher makes a composite list by asking each group to contribute a new word, until all the *k* words have been found. Then the students, in their groups, classify the *k* words by their spellings. One list would be all the words where the *k* sound is spelled with the letter *c* and another list with *k*.

As a final activity, groups try to find patterns in the spellings. They might notice, for example, that *c* is used for the *k* sound at the beginning of words if the next letter is a consonant or one of the vowels, *a, o,* or *u,* as in *club, cab, cone,* or *cube*. On the other hand, the letter *k* is used at the beginning of words when the next letter is *e* or *i,* as in *keep* and *kind*.

Students can identify both the patterns and the reasons for them. Some students might realize, for instance, that when *e* or *i* follows a *c,* the *c* no longer has the *k* sound. Instead, it sounds like *s,* as in *cent*. As students discuss these insights, they bring to a conscious level how the graphophonic system works, how the sounds and spellings match up. They do this in the context of a meaningful activity, not with a worksheet. The resulting insights can help them in both their reading and their spelling.

Lesson Three

Students are given a passage with some words deleted. As they discuss this Cloze exercise and suggest words for the blanks, they realize that they can figure out many answers, even with no graphophonic cues. This helps them understand that they don't need to be so dependent on graphophonics as they read. (See Chapter Eight for a discussion of the differences between teaching strategy lessons on graphophonics and teaching phonics and phonemic awareness directly.)

Strategy Lessons: Using Syntactic Cues

Lesson One

One syntax lesson is for students having trouble reading dialogue. These students might work in small groups to rewrite a play as a story. As they do this, they must decide how to rewrite the dialogue. They could choose to use direct speech or indirect speech:

Direct—Sara said, "How is he?"
Indirect—Sara asked how he was.

This activity makes students more aware of the differences in syntax between the two kinds of speech. This could be especially helpful for English-language learners if they are beginning to acquire these structures in their oral language.

Lesson Two

Another strategy lesson that focuses on syntax has students work in pairs or small groups in a Cloze activity in which they fill in missing words from a story. The teacher creates the text by finding a good short story or content text and taking out some of the function words, like prepositions and conjunctions, and some of the content words, like nouns and verbs. The students should talk through what words they think go in the blanks and why they chose those words. Once all the groups are finished, the teacher can have them compare their stories with the original text. Students may find they did a better job than the author!

A way to help students focus on syntax in this activity is to ask them which blanks were easy to fill in and which ones were hard. Generally, native English speakers will find the blanks for function words easier to decide on. There are only a few prepositions or conjunctions in our language, but many nouns and verbs. However, second language learners often find function words, especially prepositions, difficult.

Students can discuss the clues they used to decide what kind of word should go in each blank. This activity helps them understand that the little function words play an important role in helping readers predict what is coming next. Students often realize that they can substitute different content words in a story without losing the meaning.

Strategy Lessons: Using Semantic Cues

Lesson One

Passages with key words deleted can also be used to create lessons that focus on semantics. For example, a teacher might delete the conjunctions from a short text. Students working in groups can decide what words go in the blanks. In this process, they become more conscious of the importance of connecting words that show the relationships between ideas. Or teachers might delete the pronouns and help readers see that they can use cues from earlier in the text to predict which pronouns will occur.

Lesson Two

One especially useful vocabulary-building strategy for teachers to use when working with English learners is that of drawing on what they know in their first language and applying that knowledge to English. Spanish speakers, for example, would not find words like *observe, predict,* or *estimate* difficult to understand in English once they connect those words to *observar, predecir,* and *estimar,* commonly-used words in their native language. This strategy works especially well with a language like Spanish, which has many cognates. If teachers can help Spanish speakers draw on what they know and apply that when they read, those students will find that they know many more words than they thought they did. (See Chapter Eight for a discussion of the problems with some other approaches to teaching vocabulary.)

Strategy lessons can help students become more proficient readers by making them aware of the processes they use as they construct meaning.

Effective teachers base the lessons on their assessment of students' use of background knowledge and the three cueing systems. These teachers also know that although strategy lessons can be very useful, they are only a small part of an effective program. Students need good books and time to read so that they can put the strategies to use.

Conclusion

Teachers who follow the Checklist for Effective Reading Instruction use both informal and formal assessments to determine how well readers are using all three cueing systems to construct meaning from texts. Results from miscue analysis often show patterns, such as those reflected in Figure 6–1. Many troubled readers rely heavily on graphophonics and fail to use syntactic and semantic information. Often, they are focused on pronouncing individual words rather than on making sense of text. This is especially true of English-language learners. Miscue analysis can help teachers plan instruction for troubled readers. Teachers can build on students' strengths and also provide strategy lessons to strengthen their use of the cueing systems.

However, in classes that follow effective reading instruction, strategy lessons are simply an extra boost. In such classes, students come to value reading. They learn to read by reading a variety of interesting texts. They also have many opportunities to share their responses to reading. When students talk and write about what they have read, they focus more fully on meaning. They become less concerned with getting the words right and more concerned with sharing stories and content information. In the next chapter, we consider how talking and writing about texts promotes effective reading instruction.

Talking and Writing About Reading

Checklist Questions This Chapter Addresses

Question 10: Do students have opportunities to talk about what they have read, making connections between the reading and their own experiences?

Question 11: Do students revise their individual understandings of texts in response to the comments of classmates?

Question 12: Is there evidence that students' writing is influenced by what they read?

In this chapter, we discuss the last three questions on the Checklist for Effective Reading Instruction. These questions highlight the importance of writing and talk in the development of reading proficiency.

Talk in Mike's Classroom

Socially, Mario has very positive relations with the other students in his class. Most of his friends are of Mexican descent, too . . . As far as his academic achievement, Mario sees himself as an average student, getting Bs and Cs. He is an avid reader and is currently doing a special project for the teacher, recording the text of a variety of Spanish picture books onto cassette tapes for the class listening center. This will allow other students to hear a native Spanish speaker reading a text and to follow along with the book. The project is designed to help Mario continue to work on his reading/presentation skills in his primary language, which will in turn be useful as he acquires and uses English.

The above section was taken from a case study written by Mike, a graduate student whom we introduced in the Introduction. Above, Mike is describing a student he had in fourth grade. Mike has studied both reading and English-language development in his graduate work, and then applied theory to practice in his classroom. Mike's classroom is full of rich language experiences. Students are given many opportunities to read and then talk and write about their reading. Mike describes his classroom approach:

> The classroom is a student-centered learning community, where students are accepted where they are developmentally. The teacher takes on the role of facilitator or mediator, fostering a risk-free learning environment with high expectations for each student and the belief that every student will be successful. While the teacher realizes the curricular expectations for the students in fourth grade, students choose topics that they would like to study with the teacher weaving the grade level skills/expectations into those topics through an integrated thematic teaching approach. Literature studies are at the core of all themes, whether they be centered around a social studies topic like U.S. history or a science-related theme like oceanography.

The structure of the classroom requires students to participate in numerous grouping opportunities throughout the day. A lot of dialogue occurs, providing students authentic opportunities to negotiate their learning with teacher and peers.

We begin this chapter by examining the importance of talking about books. Proficient readers not only construct meaning from texts, they also revise the meanings they build as they discuss what they have read with their classmates. Teachers like Mike who follow the Checklist for Effective Reading Instruction provide students with many opportunities to talk about texts.

Developing Reading Through Talk

Reading for pleasure is often thought of as a solitary activity. Many of us think of reading a good book while sitting quietly in our favorite chair or in a lovely natural setting. In schools, however, reading is a social activity. How that social interaction takes place largely depends upon the view of reading a teacher adopts.

Teachers who base their reading instruction on the Checklist create situations in which their students can talk about what they read and relate the reading to their personal experiences. Classroom activities are organized to help students reflect on what they have read. Comprehension questions are open-ended and promote the sharing of ideas.

Hansen Questions

An activity that encourages students to talk about books and connect them to their own experiences involves the series of four simple comprehension questions formulated by J. Hansen (1989) and shown in Figure 7–1.

Hansen's Comprehension Questions
▲ What do you remember?
▲ What else would you like to know?
▲ What does it remind you of?
▲ What other things have you read that it reminds you of?

Figure 7–1 Hansen's Comprehension Questions

♦ After reading a story to the class or after a group of students finishes a story or content area reading, the teacher might begin by asking, "What do you remember?" This open-ended question allows students to respond with a word, a phrase, or a more extended comment. For example, students who hear or read "Grandfather's Journey," Allen Say's (1993) story about his Japanese grandfather who travels back and forth between Japan and the United States, might answer, "He saw red men and black men." Another student might remember how he kept songbirds, and another the effect of the war on the characters' lives. One student's answer will often stimulate a response from a classmate. English language learners can contribute what they know, be reminded of vocabulary they could not quite remember, and learn new words during this activity. Even those students with very limited English can contribute when they recall something from a story and express it in a word or two. By the time several students have responded, the teacher has often reviewed most of the key ideas and vocabulary in the text.

♦ Teachers want students to think beyond the text, and the second question, "What else would you like to know?" often prompts this kind of thinking. Students discussing "Grandfather's Journey," for example, often ask, "How did the grandfather get enough money to travel all over the United States?" or "Where did he learn English?" These questions help students get more fully involved in the text and start to ask questions about missing information.

♦ Teachers also want students to connect the text to their lives. By asking, "What does it remind you of?" teachers encourage students to make this connection. Students discussing "Grandfather's Journey" may talk about their grandparents. English-language learners may also explain that, like the narrator, they never feel completely at home in either country.

♦ One goal of reading instruction is to help students make connections among the books they read. The fourth question, "What other things have you read that it reminds you of?" helps students do this. A story like "Grandfather's Journey" might remind students of other stories about immigrants or about grandparents. Sometimes students respond by naming other stories by the same author or other stories with art by the same illustrator.

These questions encourage students to think about what they have read or heard read, talk about what they understood, and make important connections. These comprehension questions differ from those found in most teachers' guides because they are open-ended and draw upon what students know. English learners can usually succeed in saying something in English to answer these questions. They can be used for literature as well as content reading and are appropriate for all grade levels. While teachers would not want to ask all four questions every time, any of these questions is an excellent way to help students extend and revise their comprehension of a text through talking about it with the teacher and their classmates.

Literature Studies

Teachers like Mike organize their class so students have many opportunities to read and then talk and write about their reading. One way they do this is through literature studies. Figure 7–2 gives a general outline to show how a literature study is organized (Bird and Alvarez, 1987).

Literature Studies
▲ Teacher or students do a book talk.
▲ Students read the entire book on their own (they can write in their literature logs as they go along).
▲ Students meet with the teacher and respond to the book (what they liked/ disliked/found interesting/didn't understand).
▲ Teacher assigns a task based on student discussion that has the students go back to the text and find out more about the book and especially the author's craft.
▲ Students meet again with the teacher and respond to their task (this might be by writing in their literature logs or marking places in the text with Post-It notes). From this discussion, new tasks are assigned.
▲ The procedure can be repeated until students and teacher feel the book is no longer a source of interest or information.

Figure 7–2 Literature Studies

♦ Literature studies usually start with a book talk. The teacher or another student might read part of the book aloud, read the blurb on the book jacket, act out a dramatic part, or retell an interesting event. The purpose of a book talk is to advertise the book and interest students in it. Often, a teacher gives students a choice among four or five books. The teacher does a book talk on each book, and then students list their first and second choices. Teachers use this information to organize students into literature study groups.

♦ Often, students are given time to read the entire book before they begin discussions. However, a teacher may elect to assign sections of a longer book. Students can keep a "literature log" to write down things they want to remember and discuss when they meet in groups.

♦ The teacher meets with each small group after they have finished the reading. She encourages each student to contribute to the discussion. Students can refer to their literature logs for ideas of what to talk about. The teacher acts as a group member, adding ideas and observations, but not asking specific comprehension questions.

♦ The teacher takes notes as the students talk and then asks them to go back to the text and examine certain aspects of it. During this task, students focus on the techniques a successful author uses. For example, the teacher might say, "I noticed that you commented on how you liked the way the author made the characters seem real. I'd like you to go back through the story and try to find specific things the author did to describe these characters." The teacher's questions could also focus on plot, setting, theme, or other literary elements.

♦ The students reread portions of the book. They may put Post-Its on the pages that contain good examples. Then, they bring their books and notes to the next group meeting. They respond to the assignment, and they discuss other things they noticed. The teacher may ask them to go back and look at other aspects of the book. The teacher always tries to make the assignments in response to things students bring up.

♦ The groups continue to meet as long as they find interesting information and ideas to talk about.

Literature studies draw on what students understand and encourage readers to talk among themselves and with the teacher to revise and build their comprehension. When students do not understand parts of what they read, discussion during the meeting times with the teacher and their classmates often clears up their misunderstandings.

Literature studies also give English language learners many more opportunities to succeed. In traditional classes, a teacher might ask one student a specific question as the whole class watches. This puts pressure on any student, and especially on students who are learning English. These students must first understand the question, then they must know the answer to the specific question being asked, and finally, they must have the necessary vocabulary to answer in English. Literature studies, on the other hand, allow students time to read on their own and think about what they have read. They can build their understanding by talking about the book with their peers. Mike explains how he made literature studies work for Mario:

> When it came to literature studies, I had Mario participate just like the rest of the students. He was provided with Spanish texts when available, but at times it meant that Mario would have to find a group where he would follow along in the text as his group read to him, using a Shared Reading Approach. A bilingual member of his group would offer a kind of translated summary of what the group had read to the point where they had stopped. Additionally, if I did not have a Spanish version of the book his group was reading, I would try to give Mario a Spanish book that would be similar in content to what he was reading in his group. In this way, Mario was getting content in both languages and peer support for English. Further, his involvement in the group allowed him to interact with native English speakers.

The extra efforts Mike makes allowed Mario and Mike's other limited-English-proficient students to participate in literature studies. Even when Mario can't read the text on his own, he can enter into the social interaction and offer his ideas and opinions. His teacher and his classmates know that Mario can read in Spanish, and they fully expect that soon he will read in English as well. Mario could not participate in this way if Mike simply asked him comprehension questions in English. He would probably become frustrated and not attempt to engage in English reading.

Literature Circles

A variation on a literature study is a literature circle (Short, et al., 1996; Short and Klassen, 1994). Literature circles are not as structured as literature studies and allow more flexibility. Students meet in groups to talk about books they have read, but the students do not all have to be reading the same book. Instead, they all read books organized around the same topic. The discussion, then, usually focuses initially on the topic or theme. Students may still be asked to go back and look at the way the different writers created certain effects. For example, they might look at how the writers created mood through setting in different stories, and then make a comparison-contrast chart to show the results.

The books used in a literature circle are called a "text set." Often, text sets are groups of literature and or content books that go together logically. Sometimes, teachers combine genres, but other times take one genre to show variety within it. For example, students might look at a text set of poetry that includes different types of poetry.

A text set might be a group of books by one author, a group of books about grandparents and grandchildren, a group of books that tell stories of cultural celebrations, or a group of texts, including literature and content books, about seeds. To give readers an idea of the variety of possibilities for text sets, Figure 7–3 lists text set topics that teachers we have worked with have used.

Using text sets has many benefits:

♦ Teachers can group books that include different difficulty levels. This is especially important in classes with English language learners. Students can read books appropriate for them and still contribute fully in the group discussion.

♦ Because texts sets are organized around themes or topics, the same vocabulary is repeated naturally, and English learners can develop both their English proficiency and their reading proficiency as they read and talk about the texts.

♦ Students develop concepts in depth and broaden their perspectives as they read and share books related to a common theme.

♦ Students can do many different kinds of activities in response to reading the books in a text set. For example, they can compare and contrast the various books in the text set. Such activities encourage students to think about how texts are the same and how they are different. Francisco had students compare a content book they had read in Spanish, *En aguas profundas* (García-Moliner, 1993), with one that covered similar content in English, *The Mighty Ocean* (Berger, 1996). His students did this by drawing a Venn diagram. This visual representation helped all his students, and especially his English language learners, by providing a visual representation of similarities and differences.

Literature studies and literature circles help students make connections

Text Set Topics
▲ Grandparents and grandchildren
▲ Stories about valuing memories and keepsakes
▲ New baby in the family
▲ Native Americans in the Southwest
▲ Native American folklore
▲ Folk stories of different ethnic groups
▲ "Cinderella" stories from different cultures
▲ Versions of "Three Billy Goats Gruff," "The Little Red Hen," "Cinderella," "The Three Little Pigs," "Little Red Riding Hood"
▲ Stories about migrant children
▲ Immigrant stories
▲ Stories from the South
▲ Alphabet books
▲ Counting books
▲ Plants and plant growth
▲ Seeds
▲ Butterflies
▲ Insects
▲ Recycling
▲ The ocean
▲ Conserving the environment
▲ Nutrition
▲ The life cycle
▲ The solar system
▲ Space travel
▲ Colonial U.S. history
▲ The Civil War
▲ Slavery in the United States
▲ The 1960s and the civil rights movement
▲ Kwanzaa
▲ Multicultural holidays

Figure 7–3 Text Set Topics

between what they read and their personal experiences. Students also develop a fuller understanding of what they have read by talking about the events and ideas in the stories and content area books with their classmates. As they listen to classmates, they revise their own understandings and add details they had overlooked.

Reflecting Reading in Writing

Effective reading programs should be coupled with good writing programs. It's hard to become a good writer without doing lots of reading. Reading provides the comprehensible input students need to acquire high levels of literacy. Students' writing shows teachers what they have acquired through reading. The last question on the Checklist considers the connection between reading and writing. Teachers who follow the Checklist help students connect their reading with their writing.

With guidance from teachers, students learn to draw on their reading as they write. The writing raises students' awareness of different aspects of texts, from the writing techniques authors use to how they spell and punctuate words. In the following sections, we share three classroom examples that show how students' writing can reflect what they have learned through reading.

High School Poetry Book

Tom, a high school English teacher in Michigan, encourages students in his Transitional English course to read relevant literature and respond to it. The students in Tom's class read *Children of the River* (Crew, 1989), a teen novel about a Cambodian girl's adjustment to living in the United States, attending high school, and coping with the challenges of living between cultures. As part of the discussion of this book, Tom and his students focused on the poem the main character writes about the horror of the Cambodian genocide and leaving her country, also known as Kampuchea. The immigrant students in Tom's class, many of whom were refugees, showed so much interest in the discussion that it led to the publication of a class book of poems about immigrant experiences, *A Literary Collection* (Thomas, 1998).

By writing their own poetry, Tom's students share their struggles and longing for their homeland. In Figure 7–4, Renee tells readers that she is "far away now . . . from my dearest people" and that "The day I left you was the saddest day of my life . . . ." Maya tells how much she misses her native Yugoslavian people and how she "can't bring them back" (see Figure 7–5). Ronak proudly tells readers that his native India is "the land of us and me" (Figure 7–6). These examples show how reading one relevant piece of literature led Tom's students to reflect on the difficulty of leaving their homelands and their appreciation for their native countries.

IRAQ

Oh Iraq, my lovely mother, my sweet home
Do you know how much I miss you?
And how I wish to see you one day
Even for only a short time
I am far away now from you
From my dearest people

The day I left you was the saddest day of my life
The day I'll meet you will be the happiest day of my life
I hope that day will come shortly
I don't know why I left you
I left my sweetest times
I don't know why I left my dearest friend
I don't know when I'll meet you again, Baghdad
I dream of you day and night
You are everything for me
You are the country in which I was raised
I always thought you were the place
I was going to die
If you ask me about Baghdad
I'll talk too much.

—Renee Ascie

HOMELAND

I had a beautiful life there
For nine beautiful years
Kids to play with
People to laugh with
But it's all gone now
And it's never coming back

I can't bring them back
But I can make the best
Of where I am
Right now

This new place I live makes me
Feel like I'm home
But it's still
Not the same
Because my Yugoslavia is far, far away
Far away from my new home

—Maya Gokovic

Figure 7–4

Figure 7–5

Reading and Writing in the Intermediate Grades

Mike, the teacher we discussed at the beginning of this chapter, sees his students' reading reflected in their writing all the time. Since his classroom is filled with books, and students are reading and talking about their reading daily, they naturally show evidence of that reading in their writing. It appears in their journal entries and in the stories they write and then share during whole-class sessions called the Author's Chair. The Author of the day sits in a special chair and reads his or her work. Other students make comments, ask questions, and suggest possible additions or revisions.

INDIA

I love my India.
India is a land of love and peace.
It's the land of culture and the land of being free.
This is the land of us and me.

Even this new place is a place to be free.
I miss my India even if it's not free.
But when I go back,
A lot of people want to come with us.
But I tell the people,
It's freer over here than there.

North, South, East, or West
India is the Best.

—Ronak Patel

Figure 7–6

This year, Mike is responsible for writers workshop for all one hundred fifth graders at his school. Students rotate from other homerooms into his classroom for about an hour a day. With his own class, Mike does writers' workshop and literature studies. A key goal for Mike is to have students connect their reading to their writing and to be sure that students have experiences with different genres. To track the kinds of writing students do, Mike has created a "Kinds of Writing Checklist" that students put on the cover of their writing folder. Figure 7–7 shows the cover of Ruby's folder. So far this year, she has written and published in three categories: Autobiography or Biography, Poetry, and Fable or Fairy Tale. As the year progresses, Ruby, a Punjabi/English speaker, will include the other genres listed on the checklist.

In Mike's class, the student writing also shows that they have read widely within each genre. For example, he has collected a text set of poetry so his students can read and discuss a variety of poetry, including *The D- Poems of Jeremy Bloom* (Korman and Korman, 1992) and *Hey World, Here I Am!* (Little and Truesdell, 1989), to help them see that all poetry

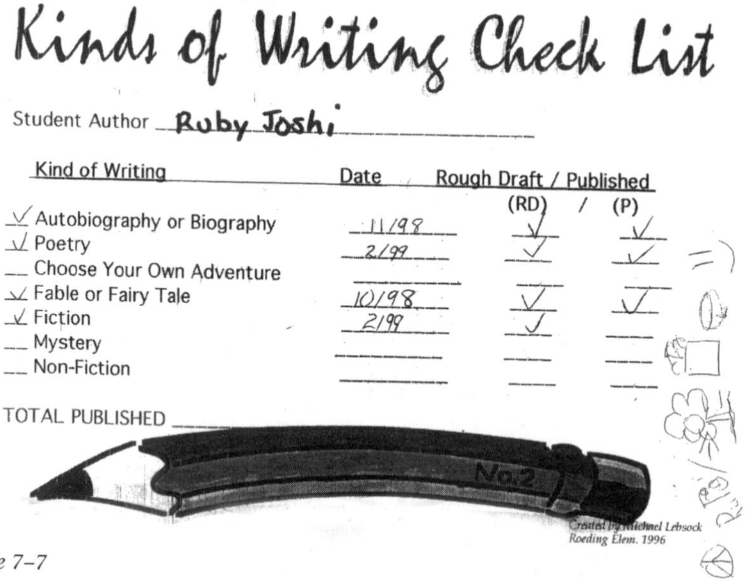

Kinds of Writing Check List

Student Author Ruby Joshi

Kind of Writing	Date	Rough Draft (RD)	Published (P)
✓ Autobiography or Biography	11/98	✓	✓
✓ Poetry	2/99	✓	✓
__ Choose Your Own Adventure			
✓ Fable or Fairy Tale	10/98	✓	✓
✓ Fiction	2/99	✓	
__ Mystery			
__ Non-Fiction			

TOTAL PUBLISHED ____

No. 2

Created by Michael Lebsock
Roeding Elem. 1996

Figure 7–7

does not have to rhyme. He wants his students to understand that poetry can "help them find their own voices." Ruby's folder has a section called "Ruby's Poetry," which reflects the variety of poetry she has read. Figure 7–8 shows two different pieces in Ruby's book.

Memories

The memories came,
All the time now,
Crowding in.
Filling her head.
They came in mists,
And clouds,
Almost revealing,
What was hidden
Behind them.
Clouds with a face,
Nearly hidden.
Clouds.
And that face.

Friendship

I want to be your friend
Forever,
And ever without break or decay.
When the hills are all flat,
And when the rivers are all
Dry,
And when it lightens and
Thunders in winter,
When Heaven and Earth
Mingle – not till then will I
Part from you.

Figure 7–8 Ruby's Poems

Mike works with his students on effective writing. Students read many books from text sets that contain examples of vivid descriptions, conflicts, and character development. Mike talks with his students about the author's point of view and techniques that writers use, such as metaphor and simile. This year, the first text set students chose included books that fifth graders were excited to read and that contained elements of writing Mike wanted to discuss: *Maniac Magee* (Spinelli, 1990), *Matilda* (Dahl, 1988), *There's a Boy in the Girl's Bathroom* (Sachar, 1987), and *Sideways Stories from Wayside School* (Sachar, 1978).

When Mike's students write, their writing shows evidence of this reading. A Vietnamese student of Mike's wrote and published an eighteen-page illustrated book entitled *Princess Lily*. Her book shows that she understands how to incorporate descriptive language in a story. Her first page reads:

> Princess Lily was a beautiful princess. She was beautiful on the inside and out. Her hair was as yellow as the blazing sun setting on the horizon.

In this story, the bad parents are reformed by the persistence of their loving princess daughter. The influence of reading fables came through in the story theme.

Students in Mike's class also write nonfiction. One particularly meaningful publication for Mike was that of a Hmong student. Ker was a struggling English learner, but a good artist. When Mike shared with the class that he was an artist and read several books with his class about different types of art in the Art for Children series (Raboff, 1987, 1988), Ker's interest in writing a book was born. His book, *Painting*, reflected his connection with Mike as an artist, his artistic ability, and his desire to communicate in English. Ker explains all this in his book:

> Ker's teacher taught them to paint very well.
> The teacher became a famous artist in 1972.
> There are different styles.
> One is cubism, realism, impressionism, abstract, and pointillism.

Much of the writing reflects reading done during content-area studies. Since Mike uses an integrated thematic instruction approach to cover curriculum requirements, he collects text sets around the theme, and his students read many content-area texts. Recently, Mike and his student teacher, Anne, linked required earth science and life science requirements into the study of landforms and environments/biomes. In groups, students chose environments/biomes they were interested in and became experts in those areas reading widely from various resources. Each group then prepared one-page written reports on the animals and landforms of their environment. They next created the environment artistically in sections of the room, complete with scale model animals and plants, stuffed and painted.

They prepared for an exhibit day when students from other classes and family members came for classroom tours. Visitors moved from the Arctic to the tropical rainforest and from the plains to the mountains and forests. Mike's students explained how the different environments affected both flora and fauna. Their written reports were hung as part of their display, and students pointed out charts and key points they had written about as they made their presentations. Among the special guests to Mike and Ann's classroom were education students from Japan, who were fascinated by all the students had learned and were sharing.

Mike's students make the important reading-writing connection all the time. These connections do not happen spontaneously, but are the result of careful planning by a knowledgeable teacher who has a wide knowledge of content area texts and literature. Mike understands the writing process, and he knows his students and their needs. Above all, Mike recognizes the important role reading plays in the development of his students' writing.

Reading and Writing in the Primary Grades

Debbie is another example of a teacher working in a multilingual context who is knowledgeable about learning, literature, and her students. We shared Debbie's daily schedule in Chapter Two. Here we briefly describe her "Moonwatch" unit and show some of the examples of how her students' writing showed evidence of their reading.

Debbie read *Moon Journals* (Chancer and Rester-Zodrow, 1997), a professional book about how a teacher educator had used moon watching as a way to get her students writing, sharing, and thinking. The idea intrigued Debbie, and she wanted to try it with her young students. However, she also preferred not to impose an inquiry topic on them, but instead to have the interest come from them. When a woman from the zoo came to talk to the children about bats, the moment arrived. In the discussion about bats and going out at night, students began to ask about the moon and the stars, and so Debbie asked the children if they would like to study the moon.

Debbie's class began by carefully designing "moon journals." They used different art techniques to design unique covers. Soon, each person, including the teacher, student teachers, classroom aides, and a university researcher, came to class prepared daily with their journal. Each night, the assignment was to watch the moon and record the observation. Debbie began with the night of the new moon. When children came back reporting there was no moon, that generated many questions that would be answered throughout the unit as everyone involved observed, reported, read, and discussed.

Debbie assembled a text set of moon books, and her students read many kinds of books together, including everything from information books to literature, poetry, and Native American folklore. (See Figure 7–9 for a sampling of the moon books in Debbie's text set.) All of the readings and activities informed the group and actually increased their interest. As Debbie explained, "I've never before had an inquiry project where there was absolutely 100 percent involvement. Everyone was interested. Everyone participated. Everyone learned."

Asch, F. 1982. *Happy Birthday, Moon*. New York: Aladdin Paperbacks.

———. 1983. *Mooncake*. New York: Aladdin Paperbacks.

Baylor, B. 1982. *Moon Song*. New York: Charles Scribner's Sons.

Branley, F.M. 1986. *What the Moon Is Like*. New York: Harper Collins.

Brenner, B. 1990. *Moon Boy*. New York: Bantam.

Brown, M.W. 1948. *Goodnight, Moon*. New York: Harper Trophy.

Bruchac, J. 1996. *Between Earth and Sky*. San Diego: Harcourt Brace & Co.

Bruchac, J., and J. London. 1992. *Thirteen Moons on Turtle's Back: A Native American Year of Moons*. New York: Putnam & Grosset.

Krupp, E.C. 1993. *The Moon and You*. New York: Simon and Schuster.

Loewer, P., and J. Loewer. 1997. *The Moonflower*. Atlanta: Peachtree Publishers.

Manuel, L. 1996. *The Night the Moon Blew Kisses*. Boston: Houghton Mifflin.

Murray, M.D. 1998. *The Stars Are Waiting*. New York: Marshall Cavendish.

Simon, S. 1984. *The Moon*. New York: Simon and Schuster.

Tan, A. 1992. *The Moon Lady*. New York: Macmillan.

Turner, C. 1991. *The Turtle and the Moon*. New York: Penguin Books.

Wood, D. 1998. *Rabbit and the Moon*. New York: Simon and Schuster.

Yolen, J. 1994. *Beneath the Ghost Moon*. Boston: Little, Brown, and Co.

———. 1987. *Owl Moon*. New York: Scholastic.

Zolotow, C. 1993. *The Moon Was the Best*. New York: Greenwillow Books.

Figure 7–9 Moon Text Set

At the end of their unit the class published a book of poetry called *Moon Images* (Manning, 1998). The various poems written by the students in Debbie's multiage classroom show both their facility with language and their knowledge of the moon. One student, Michael, wrote:

Moon
The moon shines like a white quilt tonight.
I looked at the moon tonight in the glistening sky.
I love the moon . . . . . .
     moon

The moon is bulging.
Sometimes it's miniature.
But I still love the moon.
     moon

The moon disappears.
The moon comes back,
as sparkling as ever.
     moon
That is why I love the moon.

As a culminating celebration of their inquiry, Debbie's class went on a camp out. They brought along a telescope, read their poems to each other, and watched the moon. Debbie captured the students' interest with a topic they all found fascinating. The writing they produced in *Moon Images* and their other daily assignments provided evidence of all the reading they had done during the unit.

An effective reading program involves students with meaningful reading every day. Teachers like Mike and Debbie surround their students with books. They read to them and with them. They also provide daily time for independent reading. But Mike and Debbie and other effective teachers know that reading is a social act. For that reason, they also ensure that their classrooms are filled with talk and writing about the reading that their students are doing. When students have opportunities to talk and write, they can share and extend the meanings they construct during reading. Talking and writing are essential components of any effective reading program.

Conclusion

This completes our discussion of the items on the Checklist for Effective Reading Instruction. The Checklist is based on Krashen's theory of language acquisition and a sociopsycholinguistic theory of reading. We have explained these theories and then shown how the theories look in action in multilingual classrooms where reading is taught effectively.

Throughout this book, we have shared examples from a variety of teachers who teach reading in multilingual contexts. All these teachers work in different settings with different student populations. They have different resources and face different expectations from administrators, parents, and other teachers. What they have in common is that they follow a set of principles for effective teaching of reading. They know how important it is for their students to value reading and to value themselves as readers. For that reason, they immerse their students in engaging literature and content area books. They provide demonstrations of the importance of reading. Their students see them reading for pleasure as well as information. They fill their classrooms with good books and help their students choose appropriate ones. They keep their students focused on reading effectively and efficiently and teach strategy lessons when students need to strengthen their use of one or more cueing systems. Their students talk and write about their reading.

Teachers working in multilingual classrooms face real challenges. Many of their students are trying to learn to read in a language they are still developing. Often, school or district officials expect miracles. It takes time to develop proficiency in a language, and it takes even more time to become a proficient reader. Professional teachers know this, so they make every effort to use the time they have as effectively and efficiently as possible. They stress both the importance of reading and their belief that all their students will read well. Professional teachers, like those we have described in this book, also know the importance of continuing to work to improve their teaching. We hope that the guidelines we have provided and the classroom examples will help you reflect on your own classrooms and continue to work to provide the best possible teaching for all your students.

Answering the Hard Questions about Reading

Often administrators, other teachers, or parents ask hard questions about teaching reading. In this chapter, we provide information to help teachers answer some of the questions that are frequently raised.

1. What About Phonics?

Effective teachers help their students use all the cueing systems, including graphophonics. However, helping students acquire the ability to use graphophonic cues is not the same as teaching phonics directly, explicitly, and systematically. Two books and an article that provide excellent accounts of how teachers with a sociopsycholinguistic orientation incorporate graphophonics into their reading curriculums are *Looking Closely: The Role of Phonics in One Whole Language Classroom* (Mills, et al., 1992), *Teaching Phonics in Context* (Dahl, 2000), and "Phonics Instruction and Student Achievement in Whole Language First-Grade Classrooms" (Dahl et al., 1999).

♦ The key to answering questions about phonics is to help people understand the difference between phonics and graphophonics. Figure 8–1 highlights four differences.

Phonics	Graphophonics
▲ Conscious—learned as the result of direct, systematic, explicit teaching	▲ Subconscious—acquired in the process of reading
▲ The primary source of information used in decoding words	▲ One of three sources of information used in constructing meaning
▲ A prerequisite for reading	▲ A result of reading
▲ Can be tested independently of meaningful reading	▲ Can only be assessed in the context of meaningful reading

Figure 8–1 Phonics and Graphophonics   116

♦ Phonics is conscious knowledge that results from direct teaching. For example, students may be taught that in one-syllable words such as *ran*, which has the pattern consonant-vowel-consonant, the vowel has a short sound. Students who have learned phonics rules for identifying short vowels can state them. In contrast, graphophonic knowledge is subconscious. Students acquire this knowledge as they read, and they may not be able to state the rules. However, they can use this acquired knowledge to recognize words and pronounce them during oral reading.

♦ Phonics is seen as the primary source of information available to help readers decode words. When reading is seen as a process of transforming written language into oral language, it makes sense to rely heavily on phonics, since phonics rules connect written and oral language. Some reading programs for beginning readers are labeled "phonics" programs. Often, such programs claim to contain everything children need to learn how to read. For English-language learners, such programs may result in an ability to pronounce words. The problem is that students may not be able to comprehend what they read. On the other hand, when reading is seen as a process of constructing meaning, graphophonics is regarded as just one source of information a reader can use. Readers also use their background knowledge, along with syntactic and semantic cues, to make sense of texts.

♦ Phonics knowledge is seen as a prerequisite for reading. For example, when students are given decodable texts, they are given materials that contain only words they should be able to decode using the phonics rules they have been taught. This is why early books in a phonics series have words that represent very few basic patterns. Graphophonic knowledge develops as students read. Readers build up a knowledge of common patterns of sound-letter relationships. The more they read, the more patterns they are exposed to and the more they acquire. The knowledge they are building up is not conscious information they can recite, but it is information they can use to construct meaning from texts.

♦ Since phonics rules are directly taught, they can be tested. Teachers who teach the short vowel rule, for example, can test students by giving them a list of words and telling them to mark the short vowels. This testing can be based on word lists, or even nonsense words, rather than on meaningful texts. In contrast, graphophonics is not directly taught, and students cannot usually state their knowledge of patterns of letters and sounds. Since graphophonics is used to build meaning during reading, the only way to test it is by giving a student a text to read. Procedures such as miscue analysis can be used to assess students' use of the cueing systems, including graphophonics.

2. What About Phonemic Awareness?

Phonemic awareness is the ability to perceive and manipulate the sounds (phonemes) that make up words in oral language. What this means is that a child who has developed phonemic awareness can hear a word like *pan* and tell you it has three sounds. The child can say the first sound or the middle sound. She can delete the first sound to produce *an* or change the first sound and say *can*.

Phonemes are the sounds that make a meaning difference in a particular language. Phonemes may be determined by minimal pairs. For example, in English, *pan* and *ban* only differ by the first sound. One has a *p* sound, and one has a *b* sound. Since we can find this minimal pair, we can say that *p* and *b* are phonemes in English. English has about forty phonemes. Each language contains a set of sounds to convey meanings, so different languages can have different numbers of phonemes. Spanish, for example, has about twenty-two. Since phonemes are sounds that make a difference in meaning in a particular language, English-language learners face the challenge of deciding whether a sound they hear in English is a phoneme or not. Below, we discuss the problems this can cause.

The claim is that young children who have greater phonemic awareness become better readers than children who lack phonemic awareness. Tests and exercises have been developed to measure and directly teach phonemic awareness. These tests involve adding, deleting, and substituting phonemes. Of course, the students for whom these tests and exercises are most difficult are English-language learners. They are being asked to hear and rearrange sounds in a language they are still learning.

The research on phonemic awareness (PA) is not compelling. Byrne and Fielding-Barnsley (1989), for example, found the differences in students' abilities to do PA tasks diminishes over time. Kindergarten students trained in PA did better when tested in kindergarten on isolated word identification, spelling, and nonsense word reading than students who received no PA training. However, in first grade there were no differences between trained and untrained groups on word identification or spelling, and only a small advantage for the trained group in nonsense word reading. This study suggests that PA is acquired naturally as long as children are read to and have opportunities to read. It is a result of reading, not a prerequisite.

Even when students show a difference in ability to complete PA tasks, they show little difference in comprehension. McQuillan reports on a study conducted by Torgesen and Hecht (1996), in which two hundred children were identified by low scores in phoneme deletion and letter-naming tasks in kindergarten. The children were given eighty minutes of one-on-one tutorial assistance in kindergarten and first grade. At the end of this time, the group that received training in PA and phonics did much better than the group that received no assistance in the area of "word attack," which is the ability to pronounce an unfamiliar word or a nonsense word. The trained group also did somewhat better on PA tasks like phoneme blending, but the trained group did not score significantly higher on measures of reading comprehension than the group that received no one-on-one tutoring. These and other studies suggest that students develop PA as a result of reading and being read to. The studies fail to show that PA training leads to better reading comprehension.

Much of the current emphasis on PA ignores certain linguistic realities:

♦ Phonemes are affected by the context. These variations are called the allophones. For example, when you say "Cape Cod" you can feel that the *k* sound in *Cape* is produced further forward in your mouth than the *k* sound in *Cod*. Young children feel these differences that we have learned to ignore. They might not realize that the two *k*'s are considered the same sound. Take the *t* in the middle of a word like *letter*. Doesn't it sound more like a *d* than a *t*? Allophones are variations on phonemes that proficient readers have learned to ignore but that beginning readers and English-language learners may find confusing.

♦ Phonemes vary from one language to another. This makes it difficult to accurately assess bilingual children's PA. For example, in English, *d* is one phoneme and *th* is another. A minimal pair of words that differ only by these sounds are *den* and *then*. However, in Spanish, the *d* sound and the *th* sound are allophones of one phoneme. In a word like *dedo* (finger or toe) the first *d* has a *d* sound, and the second one has a *th* sound. Spanish speakers ignore this difference the same way that English speakers ignore the two *k* sounds in *Cape Cod.* In Spanish the difference between the *d* sound and the *th* sound never makes a difference in meaning.

♦ Even within a language, speakers of different dialects pronounce words differently. David is from Maine, so he pronounces *lobster* as *lobstah.* Everyone in every language speaks some dialect. Think of students from Georgia or Texas. English language learners speak a dialect of English that is flavored by their native language. Nevertheless, exercises in PA and phonics rules assume that everyone speaks a standard English.

♦ In English, many different vowel phonemes are reduced to a schwa. This is the *uh* sound you hear in the first syllable of a word like *about* or the middle syllable in *medicine.* Most PA exercises use one-syllable words, but natural language has many long words with unaccented sounds that are hard to recognize.

♦ PA exercises and tests often use nonsense words. This causes children to focus on sounds, not meaning. For second-language learners, nonsense words are especially hard because the student may not know if the word is a nonsense word or not.

♦ PA exercises and tests are abstract. Children are asked to recognize and manipulate small bits of oral language at an age when they may not have developed the concept of words.

♦ Time spent on tests and exercises of PA is time taken away from actual reading, and a great deal of research points to the importance of time for reading.

3. What About Using Readability Formulas or Decodable Texts?

We have discussed the importance of predictability in choosing texts. Reading involves making and confirming predictions by using background knowledge and the three cueing systems to construct meaning. However, other methods of analyzing texts have been developed. Figure 8–2 contrasts predictability with readability and decodability.

	Predictability	Readability	Decodability
Based on	Features of text and experience of readers	Features of texts	Previously taught phonics skills
Determined by	Knowing readers and knowing texts	Analyzing texts	Phonics skills that need to be practiced
Useful for	Helping students you know choose books	Determining degree of text difficulty	Deciding which books to use

Figure 8–2 Predictability, Readability, and Decodability

Readability

Readability formulas are based on text features, such as word length and sentence length. A common formula, for example, determines text difficulty be counting the average number of syllables in a word and the average number of words in a sentence. The result is a grade level designation for the text. Computer programs have been devised to run different readability formulas for any text. There is no scientific basis for the conversion of word and syllable count to grade levels. The assumption is that texts with shorter sentences and shorter words are easier to read. Readability formulas don't take into account readers' knowledge or interests.

We would argue that word length and sentence length are not sufficient for deciding how difficult a text might be. For example, David has a Ph.D. in linguistics, and his undergraduate degree was in English literature. He can read classical and popular literature and enjoys complex textbooks on language, spelling, and grammar. However, when he tried to read "simple" instructions telling him how to assemble a Christmas toy for his daughters, he had trouble. The words and sentences in the instructions were not long. David can't read this genre, because he lacks the background knowledge and experience to make good predictions and construct meaning from the text.

Another example comes from classroom experiences of teachers. Beginning readers often have trouble reading and comprehending simple, short words like *the* or *there*, or even *and*. Yet, most young children recognize words like *elephant*. In fact, those longer words that attract and interest children are usually easier for them to read.

Decodability

Recently, much has been written about decodable texts. Texts are considered decodable if most of the words can be decoded by phonics rules students have been taught. Early examples of decodable texts included series like the Miami Linguistic Readers, with their "Dan can fan Nan" pages. Whether or not a text is decodable depends on the phonics rules a particular group of students has been taught. Again, there is no scientific basis for determining what a decodable text is or for determining how effective such texts are in teaching children to read (Allington and Woodside-Jiron, 1998). No one has specified how many of the words have to follow the phonics rules, and no empirical studies have been carried out that compare groups of students using decodable texts with other groups using texts that do not follow a certain set of phonics rules.

Yet, the idea of decodable texts is popular, because they fit logically into a reading program in which students first learn a set of phonics rules and then practice using those rules by decoding books written to follow the rules. The biggest problem with decodable texts is that it is very difficult to write interesting stories that follow a specific set of phonics rules.

It is not that children want the easy way out when it comes to reading, either. Watson (1997) described a troubled young reader, Alvin, who was given choices about what to read after experiences with authentic literature. Alvin rejected decodable texts as being boring and too easy, and explained that he chose literature books because they were "workable"— that is, they made him want to try to read them. Alvin demonstrates why the engaging books written by children's authors are so important for all readers.

4. What About Teaching Vocabulary?

Teachers who take a sociopsycholinguistic view expect that students will acquire vocabulary as they read. These teachers don't preteach vocabulary, because they believe that increases in vocabulary come as the result of reading. It is only as they see words in a variety of contexts that students gain word knowledge. Studies of vocabulary acquisition support this view.

Krashen (1985) reports on studies by the Center for Reading that showed that students learned an average of 1.2 words per hour as a result of direct vocabulary instruction. However, students gained 15 words per hour through reading. Similarly, Elley (1998) has conducted numerous studies that show the benefits of connecting students with books. In one study, he reported that students who were English-language learners made great gains in vocabulary simply by being read to. In one study, teachers read a story three times over a seven-day period. Students were tested for vocabulary items from the story before and after the readings. When teachers read effectively, group vocabulary scores rose 40 percent. The key was finding interesting books and coaching teachers to use reading techniques, such as pointing to pictures, gesturing, and paraphrasing, without interrupting the reading, to be sure students understood the story.

Engaging students in meaningful reading leads to vocabulary acquisition. On the other hand, attempting to teach vocabulary directly raises concerns:

♦ Probably the most serious concern is that preteaching vocabulary focuses students on individual words rather than on the meaning of the whole text. Students might come to believe that doing well on vocabulary tests means they are doing well in reading.

♦ Teachers realize that most students won't know some words in any new text. Even if students succeed in sounding these words out, they have nothing in their oral vocabulary to attach the sounds to. For that reason, teachers may choose some words to preteach. However, giving students the words is not the best approach. It's hard to predict which words all the students will have problems with. Some students know all or almost all the words in any story. Studying the words before reading is not a good use of their time. For other students, so many words are new that any list just scratches the surface.

♦ Typically, teachers pick a list of words from a story and ask students to look the words up and write definitions. Many teachers have tried this, but a key problem of students' choosing definitions in a dictionary is that the definition they choose often doesn't fit the story. The word *circulation*, for example, in one reading refers to how blood travels through the body. In another it refers to traffic movement, and in still another it refers to newspaper sales.

♦ Another concern with vocabulary is about the relationship between concepts and the words we use to label those concepts. Let's take the *circulation* example used above. If we are talking about how blood travels through the body, this is an important science concept. If a teacher chooses *circulation* as a vocabulary item to preteach before assigning a chapter from the science text, students may be able to memorize a definition without developing the concept. Teachers know that students need lots of hands-on work to develop science concepts. In the same way that a teacher might be misled into thinking a student knows a word he can pronounce, a teacher may also be misled into thinking a student knows a science concept if the student can define the vocabulary term.

♦ It would seem that English language learners in particular need more work on vocabulary. In fact, many second-language students say they like spelling and vocabulary exercises, and they often do well on those tests. They study hard to memorize the definitions and the spellings. Our experience, though, is that students have trouble applying the knowledge they gain in studying these isolated word lists to the stories and content texts they read. In the same way that students can spell words correctly on a test and then misspell them in an essay, students can define words correctly on a test and then have trouble applying that knowledge as they read. We would prefer to see students spending more time in reading activities than in prereading activities, such as vocabulary study, because reading provides the comprehensible input needed for acquisition. Students will find they know many more words than they thought they did when they have read extensively on a subject.

5. What About Teaching Greek and Latin roots?

One method some teachers use to increase students' vocabulary is to teach them common Greek and Latin roots along with prefixes and suffixes. This approach seems more efficient than trying to teach one word at a time. This strategy has limitations, however. These include deciding how to break the word into its parts, recognizing prefixes or roots that change their spelling, and knowing which meaning to use.

♦ The first task is to break the word into its parts. This does not seem hard with a word like *unimaginable*, but it is more difficult with a word like *cognate*. Is it *cogn* plus *ate*, or is it *co* plus *gnate*? This example also highlights the difficulty of working with Latin and Greek roots. Most students do not know the meanings of roots like *cogn* (to know) plus *ate* (to make)—or is it *co* (with) plus *gnatus* (to be born)? Cognates are words like *sign* and *signal* that come from the same root, that are "born with" one another, but that is not easy to discover from looking at the word parts. In cases like this, teachers have to decide if it is more efficient to teach the word parts or just teach the words.

♦ Breaking words into parts is complicated by spelling changes. Prefixes like *un* seem quite stable. The spelling doesn't change when it is added to different roots. However, *in* changes its spelling to match the first letter of the root word. It changes to *il* in *illogical*, to *ir* in *irreplaceable*, and to *im* in *immovable*. Many other common prefixes are similarly hard to recognize. Roots also change their spelling. In *unimaginable*, students have to realize that *imagine* loses an *e* before *able*. In fact, a better analysis of the word would break it down even further into "un+image+ine+able," but students might have trouble building up the meaning of the whole from these parts.

♦ Word parts change both their spellings and their meanings. For example, *un* means "not" when added to adjectives (*unusual*). However, when we add *un* to a verb, it has a different meaning. If we say we will untie our shoelaces, we do not mean that we will *not* tie them. Many prefixes have more than one meaning. In can either mean "in" (inside,) or "not" (inarticulate.)

What About Reading Aloud?

Oral reading is a common activity in many classes. Teachers sit with small groups of students and have them read aloud. When a student has difficulty with a word, the teacher might supply the word or help the student sound it out. Often, other students will jump in and provide the word. Small-group instruction allows a teacher to coach individual children, but most teachers realize the problems that come with round-robin type reading groups.

♦ Students get restless. Some are bored because the reading is easy for them, and their classmates' oral reading is too slow. Others are frustrated because the reading is too difficult for them. This is often the case for English language learners who are often learning English at the same time they are learning to read.

♦ While teachers work with one group, the other students have to work quietly on independent activities. Teachers struggle as they attempt to monitor the whole class and, at the same time, give individual attention to the students in the reading group.

♦ If one student is struggling, other students may start to give them words they are having trouble with. Over time, less proficient readers come to rely on the teacher or other students, instead of building up a repertoire of strategies for dealing with difficult texts.

♦ Taking turns reading aloud is a school activity. It's not how people read outside school, so it does not provide an appropriate model for students learning how to read.

For reasons like these, Harris and Hodges (1995, 222) define round-robin reading as "an outmoded practice of calling on students to read orally one after the other." In *Good-Bye Round Robin*, Opitz and Rasinsky (1998) offer twenty-five effective oral reading strategies that teachers can use to promote authentic oral reading. For example, older students might tape readings of books for younger students. In one school, fifth graders even sold their recordings to parents of the younger students for a class fund-raiser. Opitz and Rasinski explain each strategy clearly and offer extensions on the activities and literature to use for each. Their approach is an excellent alternative to round-robin reading.

These are six of the most common questions we encounter as we talk about reading. We hope the information we have provided here will help supply you with answers if administrators, colleagues, or parents raise these tough questions. However, we are confident that teachers who develop effective ways of teaching reading will have the best answer of all: students who can read well.

Professional References

Allington, R, S. Guice, K. Baker, N. Michaelson, and S. Li. 1995. "Access to Books: Variations in Schools and Classrooms." *The Language and Literacy Spectrum* 5: 23–35.

Allington, R. and H. Woodside-Jiron. 1998. "Decodable Text in Beginning Reading: Are Mandates and Policy Based on Research?" *ERS Spectrum*. Albany: National Research Center on English Learning and Achievement.

Berliner, D. and B. Biddle. 1995. *The Manufactured Crisis*. New York: Addison Wesley.

Bialostok, S. 1992. *Raising Readers: Helping Your Child to Literacy*. New York: Penguin.

Bird, L. and L. Alvarez. 1987. "Beyond Comprehension: The Power of Literature Study for Language Minority Students." *Elementary ESOL Education News* 10 (1): 1–3.

Byrne, B. and R. Fielding-Barnsley. 1989. "Phonemic Awareness and Letter Knowledge in the Child's Acquisition of the Alphabetic Principle." *Journal of Educational Psychology* 85: 104–111.

Chancer, J. and Rester-Zodrow. 1997. *Moon Journals*. Portsmouth, N.H.: Heinemann Educational Books.

Collier, V. 1992. "A Synthesis of Studies Examining Long-Term Language-Minority Student Data on Academic Achievement." *Bilingual Research Journal* 16 (1 & 2): 187–212.

———. 1995. "Acquiring a Second Language for School." *Directions in Language and Education* 1 (4).

Collier, V. and W. Thomas. 1996. "Effectiveness in Bilingual Education." Paper presented at the National Association of Bilingual Education, Orlando, Fla.

Cummins, J. 1996. *Negotiating Identities: Education for Empowerment in a Diverse Society*. Ontario, Calif.: California Association of Bilingual Education.

1981. "The Role of Primary Language Development in Promoting Educational Success for Language Minority Students." In *Schooling and Language Minority Students: A Theoretical Framework*. Los Angeles: Evaluation, Dissemination and Assessment Center, California State University, Los Angeles (3–49).

Dahl, K. 2000. *Teaching Phonics in Context*. Portsmouth,N.H.: Heinemann, 2000.

Day, F. 1997. *Latina and Latino Voices in Literature*. Portsmouth, N.H.: Heinemann.

Dahl, Karin, Patricia Scharer, Lori Lawson, and Patricia Grogan. 1999. "Phonics Instruction and Student Achievement in Whole Language First-Grade Classrooms." *Reading Research Quarterly* 34 (3): 312–341.

Dressman, M. "On the Use and Misuse of Research Evidence: Decoding Two States' Reading Initiatives." *Reading Research Quarterly* 34 (3): 258–285.

Education, U.S. Department of, and Office of Civil Rights. 1996. "1996 State Summaries of Elementary and Secondary School Civil Rights Survey." Washington, D.C.: National Library of Education.

Elley, W. 1991. "Acquiring Literacy in a Second Language: The Effect of Book-Based Programs." *Language Learning* 41 (2): 403–439.

———. 1998. *Raising Literacy Levels in Third World Countries: A Method that Works.* Culver City: Language Education Associates.

Elley, W. and D. Foster. 1996. "Sri Lanka Books in Schools Pilot Project: Final Report." London: International Book Development.

Elley, W. and F. Mangubhai. 1983. "The Impact of Reading on Second Language Learning." *Reading Research Quarterly* 19: 53–67.

Feitelson, D., and Z. Goldstein. 1986. "Patterns of Book Ownership and Reading to Young Children in Israeli School-Oriented and Nonschool-Oriented Families." *Reading Teacher* 39: 924–930.

Fix, M. and J.S. Passel. 1994. *Immigration and Immigrants: Setting the Record Straight.* Washington, D.C.: The Urban Institute.

Freeman, Y. and D. Freeman. 1998. *ESL/EFL Teaching: Principles for Success.* Portsmouth, N.H.: Heinemann.

Freeman, Y. S. and D. Freeman. 1997. *Teaching Reading and Writing in Spanish in the Bilingual Classroom.* Portsmouth, N.H.: Heinemann.

Goodman, D. 1999. *The Reading Detective Club.* Portsmouth, N.H.: Heinemann.

Goodman, K. 1993. *Phonics Phacts.* Portsmouth, N.H.: Heinemann Educational Books.

———. 1965. "Cues and Miscues in Reading: A Linguistic Study." *Elementary English* 42 (6): 635–642.

———. 1996. *On Reading.* Portsmouth, N.H.: Heinemann.

Goodman, Y. and A. Marek. 1996. *Retrospective Miscue Analysis: Revaluing Readers and Reading.* Katonah, N.Y.: Richard C. Owen.

Goodman, Y. D. Watson, and C. Burke. 1987. *Reading Miscue Inventory: Alternative Procedures.* New York: Richard C. Owen.

———. 1996. *Reading Strategies: Focus on Comprehension.* 2d ed. Katonah, N.Y.: Richard C. Owen.

Hansen, J. 1989. "Comprehension Questions to Make Reading and Writing Connections." In *Graduate Seminar in Literacy.* Fresno, Calif.

Harste, J. and L. Mikulecky. 1984. "The Context of Literacy in our Society." In *Becoming Readers in a Complex Society,* edited by A. Purves and O. Niles. Chicago, Ill.: University of Chicago Press 47–78.

Harris, T. and R. Hodges, eds. 1995. *The Literacy Dictionary.* Newark, Del.: International Reading Association.

Krashen, S. 1996. *Every Person a Reader: An Alternative to the California Task Force Report on Reading.* Culver City, Calif.: Language Education Associates.

———. 1985. *Inquiries and Insights.* Haywood, Calif.: Alemany Press.

———. 1992. *Fundamentals of Language Education.* Torrance, Calif.: Laredo

———. 1993. *The Power of Reading.* Englewood, Colo.: Libraries Unlimited.

———. 1996. *Under Attack: The Case Against Bilingual Education.* Culver City, Calif.: Language Education Associates.

———. 1999. *Condemned Without a Trial: Bogus Arguments Against Bilingual Education.* Portsmouth, N.H.: Heinemann.

———. 1999. *Three Arguments Against Whole Language and Why They Are Wrong.* Portsmouth, N.H.: Heinemann.

LeMoine, N, E. Brandlin, B. O'Brian, and J. McQuillan. 1997. "The (Print)-Rich Get

Richer: Library Access in Low-and High-achieving Elementary Schools." *California Reader* 30: 23–25.

Mace-Matluck, B., R Alexander-Kasparik, and R Queen. 1998. *Through the Golden Door: Education Approaches to Immigrant Adolescents with Limited Schooling.* McHenry, Ill.: Delta Systems.

McQuillan, J. 1998. *The Literacy Crisis: False Claims, Real Solutions.* Portsmouth, N.H.: Heinemann.

Mills, H., T. O'Keefe, and D. Stephens. 1992. *Looking Closely: The Role of Phonics in One Whole Language Classroom.* Urbana, Ill.: National Council of Teachers of English.

Morrow, L, E. O'Connor, and J. Smith. 1990. "Effects of a Story Reading Program on the Literacy Development of At-risk Kindergarten Children." *Journal of Reading Behavior* 22: 255–275.

Opitz, M. and T. Rasinski. 1998. *Good-bye Round Robin: Twenty-five Effective Oral Reading Strategies.* Portsmouth, N.H.: Heinemann.

Ramos, F. and S. Krashen. 1998. "The Impact of One Trip to the Public Library: Making Books Available May Be the Best Incentive for Reading." *The Reading Teacher* 51 (7: 614–615.

Raz, I. and P. Bryant. 1990. "Social Background, Phonological Awareness, and Children's Reading." *British Journal of Developmental Psychology* 8: 209–225.

Rosenblatt, L. 1978. *The Reader, the Text, the Poem: The Transactional Theory of the Literary Work.* Carbondale, Ill.: Southern Illinois University Press.

Samway, Katherine, Gail Whang, and Mary Pippitt. 1995. *Buddy Reading: Cross Age Tutoring in a Multicultural School.* Portsmouth, N.H. Heinemann.

Short, K., Jerome Harste, and C. Burke. 1996. *Creating Classrooms for Authors and Inquirers.* Portsmouth, N.H.: Heinemann.

Short, K.G. and C. Klassen. 1994. "Literature Circles: Hearing Children's Voices." In *Literature Across the Curriculum: Making It Happen,* edited by B. Cullinan. Newark, Del.: International Reading Association.

Smith, C., B. Constantino, and S. Krashen. 1996. "Differences in Print Environment for Children in Beverly Hills, Compton, and Watts." *Emergency Librarian* 24 (4): 8–9.

Smith, F. 1983. *Essays into Literacy: Selected Papers and Some Afterthoughts.* Portsmouth, N.H.: Heinemann.

———. 1985. *Reading Without Nonsense.* 2d ed. New York: Teachers College Press.

Torgesen, J. and S. Hecht. 1996. "Preventing and Remediating Reading Disabilities: Instructional Variables that Make a Special Difference for Special Students." In *The First R: Every Child's Right to Read,* edited by M. Graves, P. Van Den Broek, and B. Taylor. New York: Teacher's College Press.

Ujiie, J. and S. Krashen. 1996. "Comic Book Reading, Reading Achievement, and Pleasure Reading Among Middle Class and Chapter I Middle School Students." *Reading Improvement* 33: 50–54.

Watson, D. 1997. "Beyond Decodable Texts-Supportive and Workable Literature." *Language Arts* 74: 636–643.

Wilde, Sandra. 2000. *Miscue Analysis Made Easy: Building on Students Strengths.* Portsmouth, N.H. Heinemann.

Worthy, J. 1996. "Removing Barriers to Voluntary Reading for Reluctant Readers: The Role of School and Classroom Libraries." *Language Arts* 73: 483–492.

Literature References

Ada, A. 1991. *Días y días de poesía*. Carmel: Hampton Brown, 1991.

———. 1997. *Gathering the Sun*. New York: Lothrop, Lee & Shepard.

———. 1993. *My Name Is María Isabel*. New York: Atheneum Books.

Ada, A., V. Harris, and L. Hopkins. 1993. *A Chorus of Cultures: Developing Literacy Through Multicultural Poetry*. Carmel, Calif.: Hampton-Brown Books.

Almada, P. 1993. *El mosquito*. Crystal Lake, Ill.: Rigby.

———. 1993. *La mosca*. Crystal Lake, Ill.: Rigby.

Altman, L. 1993. *Amelia's Road*. New York: Lee & Low Books Inc.

Anzaldúa, G. 1993. *Friends from the Other Side*. San Francisco: Children's Book Press.

Asch, F. 1982. *Happy Birthday, Moon*. New York: Aladdin Paperbacks.

———. 1997. *Moonbear's Books, Invitations to Literacy*. Boston: Houghton Mifflin.

———. 1983. *Mooncake*. New York: Aladdin Paperbacks.

———. 1995. *Water*. New York: Scholastic.

Asimov, I. 1999. *Why Are the Whales Vanishing?* Boston: Houghton Mifflin.

Baylor, B. 1982. *Moon Song*. New York: Charles Scribner's Sons.

Berger, M. 1996. *The Mighty Ocean*. New York: Newbridge Communications Inc.

———. 1999. *Oil Spill!* Boston: Houghton Mifflin.

Blos, J. 1987. *Old Henry*. New York: Morrow.

Bradman, T. 1998. *Michael*. Pomfret, Vt.: Trafalgar Square.

Branley, F.M. 1986. *What the Moon Is Like*. New York: Harper Collins.

Brenner, B. 1990. *Moon Boy*. New York: Bantam.

Brown, M.W. 1948. *Goodnight, Moon*. New York: Harper Trophy.

Browne, A. 1988. *I Like Books*. London: Julia MacRae Books.

Bruchac, J. 1996. *Between Earth and Sky*. San Diego: Harcourt Brace & Company.

Bruchac, J. and J. London. 1992. *Thirteen Moons on Turtle's Back: A Native American Year of Moons*. New York: Putnam & Grosset.

Bunting, E. 1988. *How Many Days to America?* Boston: Clarion Books.

Canizares, S. 1998. *Butterfly*. New York: Scholastic.

Canizares, S. and P. Chanko. 1998. *What Do Insects Do?* New York: Scholastic.

Canizares, S. and M. Reid. 1998. *Where Do Insects Live?* New York: Scholastic.

Cappellini, M. 1993. *La mariquita*. Crystal Lake, Ill.: Rigby.

Carden, M. and M. Cappellini. 1997. *Soy de dos lugares: Poesía juvenil*. Crystal Lake, Ill.: Rigby.

———. 1997. *I Am of Two Places: Children's Poetry*. Crystal Lake, Ill.: Rigby.

Carle, E. 1989. *The Mixed-Up Chameleon*. New York: Scholastic.

———. 1984. *The Very Busy Spider*. New York: Scholastic.

———. 1969. *The Very Hungry Caterpillar*. Cleveland: The World Publishing Co.

Chermayeff, I. 1997. *Fishy Facts*. Boston: Houghton Mifflin.

Chesworth, M. 1996. *Archibald Frisby*. New York: Farrar, Strauss and Giroux Inc.

Cohen, B. 1983. *Molly's Pilgrim*. New York: Lothrop, Lee & Shepard Books.

Cohen, M. 1977. *When Will I Read?* New York: Dell Publishing Co.

Cole, A. 1993. *Color*. New York: Dorling Kindersley.

Cooper, D. 1999. *Soar to Success*. Boston: Houghton Mifflin.

Cowcher, H. 1999. *Antarctica*. Boston: Houghton Mifflin.

Crew, L. 1989. *Children of the River*. New York: Dell Publishing.

D'Atri, A. 1993. *El amigo nuevo, Nuestro Barrio*. Orlando: Harcourt Brace Jovanovich.

Dahl, R. 1988. *Matilda*. New York: Scholastic.

Dooley, N. 1991. *Everyone Cooks Rice*. New York: Carolrhoda Books, Inc.

———. 1993. *Todo el mundo cocina arroz*. New York: Scholastic.

Dussling, J. 1998. *Bugs! Bugs! Bugs!* New York: DK Publishing Co.

DuTemple, L. 1999. *Whales*. Boston: Houghton Mifflin.

Ehlert, L. 1990. *Fish Eyes: A Book You Can Count on*. New York: Trumpet.

Esbensen, B. 1999. *Baby Whales Drink Milk*. Boston: Houghton Mifflin.

Ethan, E. and M. Bearanger. 1999. *Coral Reef Hunters*. Boston: Houghton Mifflin.

Facklam, M. 1999. *Bugs for Lunch*. New York: Scholastic.

Florian, D. 1998. *Insectlopedia*. New York: Scholastic.

Fox, M. 1997. *Whoever You Are*. San Diego: Harcourt Brace.

———. 1985. *Wilfrid Gordon McDonald Partridge*. Brooklyn, N.Y.: Kane-Miller.

Freedman, R. 1980. *Immigrant Kids*. New York: Scholastic Inc.

Friedman, I. 1984. *How My Parents Learned to Eat*. Boston: Houghton Mifflin.

García-Moliner, G.1993. *En aguas profundas, Celebremos la literatura*. Boston: Hougton Mifflin.

Garza, C. 1990. *Family Pictures: Cuadros de familia*. San Francisco: Children's Book Press.

———. 1996. *In My Family: En mi familia*. San Francisco: Children's Book Press.

Gibson, G. 1994. *Science for Fun: Light and Color*. Brookfield, Conn.: Copper Beech Books.

Heller, R. 1995. *Color, Color, Color, Color*. New York: Scholastic.

———. 1985. *How to Hide a Butterfly and Other Insects*. New York: Grosset and Dunlap.

Henkes, K. 1991. *Chrysanthemum*. New York: William Morrow.

Herminio Acuña, M. 1997. *Dressing with Pride*. Crystal Lake, Ill.: Rigby.

———. 1997. *Vestiimos con orgullo*. Crystal Lake, Ill.: Rigby.

Jackson, I. 1998. *The Big Bug Search*. New York: Scholastic.

Jiménez, F. 1998. *La mariposa*. Boston: Houghton Mifflin.

Karon, J. 1994. *At Home in Mitford*. New York: Penguin Books.

———. 1999. *A New Song*. New York: Penguin Books.

Keane, S. 1997. *Dear Abuelita*. Crystal Lake, Ill.: Rigby.

———. 1997. *Querida abuelita.* Crystal Lake, Ill.: Rigby.

Kite, P. 1997. *Insectos asombrosos.* Boston: Houghton Mifflin.

Knight, M. 1993. *Who Belongs Here? An American Story.* Gardiner, Maine: Tilbury House.

Korman, G. and B. Korman. 1992. *The D-Poems of Jeremy Bloom.* New York: Scholastic.

Krauss, R. 1971. *Leo the Late Bloomer.* New York: Prentice Hall.

Krupp, E.C. 1993. *The Moon and You.* New York: Simon and Schuster.

Lambert, D. 1999. *The Kingfisher Young People's Book of Oceans.* New York: Scholastic.

Levinson, R. 1987. *Mira, cómo salen las estrellas.* Madrid, Spain: Ediciones Altea.

———. 1985 *Watch the Stars Come Out.* New York: E.P. Dutton.

Little, J. and S. Truesdell. 1989. *Hey World, Here I Am!* New York: Harper Trophy.

Loewer, P. and J. Loewer. 1997. *The Moonflower.* Atlanta: Peachtree Publishers.

Lowry, L. 1989. *Number the Stars.* New York: Dell Publishing.

Maitland, K. 1997. *A Surprise for Monica.* Crystal Lake, Ill.: Rigby.

———. 1997. *Una sorpresa para Mónica.* Crystal Lake, Ill.: Rigby.

Manning, D., ed. 1998. *Moon Images.* Fresno: Room 4, Dailey School.

Manuel, L. 1996. *The Night the Moon Blew Kisses.* Boston: Houghton Mifflin.

McGovern, A. 1976. *Sharks.* New York: Scholastic.

Murray, M.D. 1998. *The Stars Are Waiting.* New York: Marshall Cavendish.

Nguyen, A. and P. Abello. 1997. *Nuestro viaje hacia la libertadad.* Crystal Lake, Ill.: Rigby.

———. 1997. *Our Trip to Freedom.* Crystal Lake, Ill.: Rigby.

Oppenheim, J. 1996. *Have You Seen Bugs?* New York: Scholastic.

Oz, C. 1988. *How Is a Crayon Made?* New York: Scholastic.

———. 1993. *¿ Cómo se hace un crayón?* New York: Scholastic.

Pallotta, J. 1998. *The Butterfly Counting Book.* New York: Scholastic.

———. *The Icky Bug Counting Book.* New York: Scholastic.

———. 1986. *The Icky Bug Alphabet Book.* New York: Scholastic.

———. 1986. *The Ocean Alphabet Book.* New York: Trumpet.

Pascal, F. *Sweet Valley High Series.* New York: Bantam Books.

Patterson, K. 1994. *Flip-Flop Girl.* Dutton: New York.

Perry, S. 1995. *If . . .* Venice, Calif.: Children's Library Press.

Pfister, M. 1994. *El pez arco iris.* New York: Ediciones Norte-Sur.

Polacco, P. 1988. *The Keeping Quilt.* New York: Simon and Schuster Books for Young Children.

Puncel, M. 1997. *El amigo nuevo.* Boston: Houghton Mifflin.

Raboff, E. 1987. *Leonardo Da Vinci, Art for Children.* New York: Harper & Row Publishers.

———. 1987. *Pablo Picasso, Art for Children.* New York: Harper & Row Publishers.

———. 1988. *Vincent Van Gogh, Art for Children.* New York: Harper & Row Publishers.

Reid, M, and B. Chessen. 1998. *Bugs, Bugs, Bugs, Science:* New York: Scholastic.

Sabin, F. 1985. *Whales and Dolphins.* Mahwah, N.J.: Troll Associates.

Sachar, L. 1978. *Sideways Stories from Wayside School.* New York: Avon.

———. 1987. *There's a Boy in the Girl's Bathroom.* New York: Scholastic.

Sandved, K. 1996. *The Butterfly Alphabet*. New York: Scholastic.

Say, A. 1993. *Grandfather's Journey*. Boston: Houghton Mifflin.

———. 1997. *La jornada de abuelo*. Boston: Houghton Mifflin.

Simon, S. 1984. *The Moon*. New York: Simon and Schuster.

———. 1999. *Whales*. Boston: Houghton Mifflin.

Soto, G. 1990. *Baseball in April and Other Stories*. San Diego: Harcourt Brace Jovanovich.

———. *Buried Onions*. San Diego: Harcourt Brace.

———. 1994. *Crazy Weekend*. New York: Scholastic.

———. 1992. *Living up the Street*. New York: Dell Publications.

———. 1996. *Neighborhood Odes*. New York: Harcourt Brace.

Spinelli, J. 1990. *Maniac Magee*. New York: Scholastic.

Staub, F. 1999. *Sea Turtles*. Boston: Houghton Mifflin.

Stine, R.L. Goosebumps Series. New York: Scholastic.

Tan, A. 1992. *The Moon Lady*. New York: Macmillan.

Thomas, T. ed. 1998. *A Literary Collection*. Sterling Heights, Mich.: Sterling Heights High School.

Trapani, I. 1996. *The Itsy Bitsy Spider*. Boston: Houghton Mifflin.

Turner, C. 1991. *The Turtle and the Moon*. New York: Penguin Books.

Wainman, M. 1982. *One Elephant, Two Elephants*. Port Coquitlam, Canada: Class Size Books.

Walker, C. 1993. *Light and Color*. Cleveland: Modern Curriculum Press.

Whitney, N. 1996. *The Tiny Dot*. Boston: Houghton Mifflin.

Whittell, G. 1999. *The Story of Three Whales*. Boston: Houghton Mifflin.

Wood, D. 1998. *Rabbit and the Moon*. New York: Simon and Schuster.

Wylie, J. and D. Wylie. 1983. *Un cuento curioso de colores*. New York: Children's Press.

———. 1985. *Un cuento de peces y sus formas*. New York: Children's Press.

Yolen, J. 1994. *Beneath the Ghost Moon*. Boston: Little, Brown, and Co.

———. 1987. *Owl Moon*. New York: Scholastic.

Zolotow, C. 1993. *The Moon Was the Best*. New York: Greenwillow Books.

Index